TRACK FIBROMYALGIA

A Detailed Three Month Journal to Record Fibro Symptoms, Triggers, Medications and More.

Medjournal Essentials

A.F. White

Track Fibromyalgia

ISBN: 978-1-914297-12-0

CONTENTS

Fibromyalgia

KEEPING A SYMPTOM DIARY

Keeping a record of your symptoms can be an important part of diagnosing and managing fibromyalgia. While the main symptoms of fibromyalgia are widespread pain and fatigue, the other symptoms experienced can be different for everyone. With this in mind, there are lots of sections for recording the most common symptoms of fibromyalgia, but also boxes and sections you can personalise to help you keep track of what is important to you. You can also discuss with your doctor exactly what information they would like you to record.

Why Is It Important to Keep a Symptom Log?

There are several reasons you might wish to keep a symptom log – to aid in diagnosis, to help you and your doctor to make decisions about treatment, and to help you spot patterns and triggers.

Diagnosis & Treatment Decisions

When thinking about a diagnosis of fibromyalgia, your doctor needs to know about your symptoms over the last three months. It can be difficult to remember how things have been over time, but using a journal such as this one can help you lay out your symptoms in an easy-to-read format to help your doctor to see if you reach the diagnostic criteria. The fatigue and pain sections use the same symptom severity score and body part rating as most doctors.

If you have already been diagnosed, writing down the symptoms you are experiencing can help you reach ongoing decisions about your care. Keeping a record also helps you and your doctor decide whether medications are effective or need changing. If things get better, stay the same, or get worse after a medication change or starting a supplement or exercise regime, everyone needs to know. A log will also help you track side effects from medications you take. All this information helps you and your health-care provider make informed decisions about treatment. This journal allows you to keep all your notes and questions together and to share them easily when you go to appointments.

Patterns & Triggers

Noting what was going on around the time that symptoms happened may help you spot patterns and identify potential triggers. It may be that poor sleep, stress, a change in the temperature, or a day of high activity have contributed to a flare up. Identifying triggers could help you find ways to manage your symptoms, or to see if anything you are trying is helping or making things worse.

There are sections to record your activity levels, how many hours you slept and how refreshed you were upon waking, exercise, the weather, stress, missed meals, and a notes section to record anything that is useful to you.

Recording Your Symptoms

There are several places in this book for recording your symptoms and other important information.

Medication Tracker

If you take any medications, including prescriptions from your doctor or supplements, you can record them in this section. Each medication or supplement has its own page where you can record the dosage and frequency, note any changes to the dose and why the changes were made, and also write down any improvements you see or side effects you experience.

Questions to Ask Your Doctor

It can be difficult to remember everything you wanted to ask when you are in the consulting room. Use this section to note down any questions you have for your doctor.

Monthly Symptom Calendar

People with fibromyalgia can experience many different symptoms. We have listed some of the most common on the monthly tracking pages, but only some may apply to you, and there are spaces to add your own. There are also some common triggers such as stress, high activity and poor sleep listed. All the monthly pages are grouped together so you can easily look for trends month on month. It is quick and easy to record your symptoms each day - tick, dot, dash, colour in or strike through depending on your preference. You may want to record the severity of your symptoms using a numbered scale (e.g. 0 for no symptoms, 10 for very severe) or you can create your own visual scale using the blank boxes, you might choose different colours or use the following example. You can record your symptoms in more detail on the daily pages, but also adding the information to the monthly overview makes it quick and easy to look for patterns and to see an overall trend.

None Mild Moderate Severe

Daily Symptom Tracker

The daily pages give you an opportunity to record hours slept, the weather, fatigue, brain fog, activity levels, as well as keeping daily notes, and a detailed symptom and pain tracker.

Fatigue / Pain Levels / Cognitive Symptoms / Anxiety / Activity

Each day you have the opportunity to track fatigue, pain and other symptoms, where 0 represents no symptoms and 3 is severe, see chart below. You may discover patterns. It could be that low energy and brain fog strike together, that fatigue is always worse in the afternoon, or a high activity morning is followed by increased pain later in the day, or the next day. If it has been a particularly good or bad day, write down what happened in the notes section for future reference. There is also a blank tracker you can personalise.

Fatigue

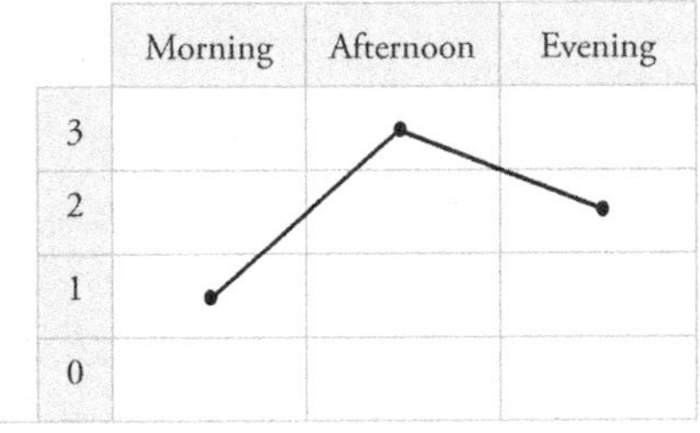

Severity Scale		
3	Severe	Life disturbing / constant
2	Moderate	Considerable symptoms / often present
1	Slight	Mild / intermittent
0	None	No problem

Pain Location & Levels

Here you can record pain you have experienced. You can shade in areas of the body, tick the boxes, or use a pain score in the chart. This chart lists the same body areas that many doctors use when reaching a diagnosis so they can quickly see how your experiences match up to their diagnostic criteria. There is a short notes section here too.

Tick Box Symptom Tracker

Quickly record symptoms you have experienced here. The most common symptoms are included, but there are also blank boxes to record your own. Either daily or at the end of the month you may wish to also record these on the monthly tracking pages so you can see trends over time. Add more detail to the notes section if needed.

One Last Thing

We are always looking to improve, and regularly review our journals to make sure they are meeting your needs. If you have a suggestion for something we can add to future revisions, want to let us know about something we do well, or something we could do better, please get in touch. We read every suggestion we receive and always appreciate your feedback.

Contact us on: customersupport@medjournalessentials.com

Medication & Supplement Tracker

Medication / Supplement Tracker

Medication & Dose	Date Started	Reason for Starting
	Date Stopped	Reason for Stopping

Changes

Date	New Dose	Reason for Change

Date	Improvements / Side Effects

Medication / Supplement Tracker

Medication & Dose	Date Started	Reason for Starting
	Date Stopped	**Reason for Stopping**

Changes

Date	New Dose	Reason for Change

Date	Improvements / Side Effects

Medication / Supplement Tracker

Medication & Dose	Date Started	Reason for Starting
	Date Stopped	Reason for Stopping

Changes

Date	New Dose	Reason for Change

Date	Improvements / Side Effects

Medication / Supplement Tracker

Medication & Dose	Date Started	Reason for Starting
	Date Stopped	Reason for Stopping

Changes

Date	New Dose	Reason for Change

Date	Improvements / Side Effects

Medication / Supplement Tracker

Medication & Dose	Date Started	Reason for Starting
	Date Stopped	Reason for Stopping

Changes

Date	New Dose	Reason for Change

Date	Improvements / Side Effects

Medication / Supplement Tracker

Medication & Dose	Date Started	Reason for Starting
	Date Stopped	**Reason for Stopping**

Changes

Date	New Dose	Reason for Change

Date	Improvements / Side Effects

Medication / Supplement Tracker

Medication & Dose	Date Started	Reason for Starting
	Date Stopped	Reason for Stopping

Changes

Date	New Dose	Reason for Change

Date	Improvements / Side Effects

Medication / Supplement Tracker

Medication & Dose	Date Started	Reason for Starting
	Date Stopped	Reason for Stopping

Changes

Date	New Dose	Reason for Change

Date	Improvements / Side Effects

Medication / Supplement Tracker

Medication & Dose	Date Started	Reason for Starting
	Date Stopped	**Reason for Stopping**

Changes

Date	New Dose	Reason for Change

Date	Improvements / Side Effects

Medication / Supplement Tracker

Medication & Dose	Date Started	Reason for Starting
	Date Stopped	**Reason for Stopping**

Changes

Date	New Dose	Reason for Change

Date	Improvements / Side Effects

Medication / Supplement Tracker

Medication & Dose	Date Started	Reason for Starting
	Date Stopped	Reason for Stopping

Changes

Date	New Dose	Reason for Change

Date	Improvements / Side Effects

Medication / Supplement Tracker

Medication & Dose	Date Started	Reason for Starting
	Date Stopped	**Reason for Stopping**

Changes

Date	New Dose	Reason for Change

Date	Improvements / Side Effects

Medication / Supplement Tracker

Medication & Dose	Date Started	Reason for Starting
	Date Stopped	Reason for Stopping

Changes

Date	New Dose	Reason for Change

Date	Improvements / Side Effects

Questions to Ask Your Doctor

Questions to Ask Your Doctor

Questions to Ask Your Doctor

Questions to Ask Your Doctor

Monthly Symptom Tracker

Month:

Number Scale: 0 is not at all 10 is most severe. Create your own visual scale: None ☐ Mild ☐ Moderate ☐ Severe ☐

	1	2	3	4	5	6	7	8	9	10	11	12	13	14	15	16	17	18	19	20	21	22	23	24	25	26	27	28	29	30	31
Pain																															
Fatigue																															
Brain Fog																															
Anxiety / Low Mood																															
Exercise																															
Poor Sleep																															
Waking Unrefreshed																															
Bladder Symptoms																															
Bowel Symptoms																															
Headache / Migraine																															
Muscle Twinges																															
Muscle Weakness																															

	1	2	3	4	5	6	7	8	9	10	11	12	13	14	15	16	17	18	19	20	21	22	23	24	25	26	27	28	29	30	31
Skin Problems																															
Loss of Appetite																															
Nausia																															
Stress																															
Numbness / Tingling																															

Month:

Number Scale: 0 is not at all 10 is most severe. Create your own visual scale: None ☐ Mild ☐ Moderate ☐ Severe ☐

	1	2	3	4	5	6	7	8	9	10	11	12	13	14	15	16	17	18	19	20	21	22	23	24	25	26	27	28	29	30	31
Pain																															
Fatigue																															
Brain Fog																															
Anxiety / Low Mood																															
Exercise																															
Poor Sleep																															
Waking Unrefreshed																															
Bladder Symptoms																															
Bowel Symptoms																															
Headache / Migraine																															
Muscle Twinges																															
Muscle Weakness																															

	1	2	3	4	5	6	7	8	9	10	11	12	13	14	15	16	17	18	19	20	21	22	23	24	25	26	27	28	29	30	31
Skin Problems																															
Loss of Appetite																															
Nausia																															
Stress																															
Numbness / Tingling																															

Month:

Number Scale: 0 is not at all 10 is most severe. Create your own visual scale: None ☐ Mild ☐ Moderate ☐ Severe ☐

	1	2	3	4	5	6	7	8	9	10	11	12	13	14	15	16	17	18	19	20	21	22	23	24	25	26	27	28	29	30	31
Pain																															
Fatigue																															
Brain Fog																															
Anxiety / Low Mood																															
Exercise																															
Poor Sleep																															
Waking Unrefreshed																															
Bladder Symptoms																															
Bowel Symptoms																															
Headache / Migraine																															
Muscle Twinges																															
Muscle Weakness																															

	1	2	3	4	5	6	7	8	9	10	11	12	13	14	15	16	17	18	19	20	21	22	23	24	25	26	27	28	29	30	31
Skin Problems																															
Loss of Appetite																															
Nausia																															
Stress																															
Numbness / Tingling																															

Daily Symptom Log

Date: ***Weather:***

Hours Slept: Insomnia? Yes ☐ No ☐

How did you feel on waking today? I felt refreshed: ☐

Slightly unrefreshed: ☐ Moderately unrefreshed: ☐ Severely unrefreshed: ☐

Did you exercise today? Yes ☐ No ☐

		Morning	Afternoon	Evening
	3			
	2			
	1			
Fatigue	0			
	3			
	2			
	1			
Pain Levels	0			
	3			
	2			
	1			
Cognitive Symptoms / Brain Fog	0			

		Morning	Afternoon	Evening
	3			
	2			
	1			
Anxiety / Low Mood	0			
	3			
	2			
	1			
Activity Levels	0			
	3			
	2			
	1			
Other	0			

Symptom Score: 0 = No problem, 1 = Slight, 2 = Moderate, 3 = Severe. See p.3

Today's Notes:

Pain Location & Levels

Shade bodies, tick boxes or use pain score.

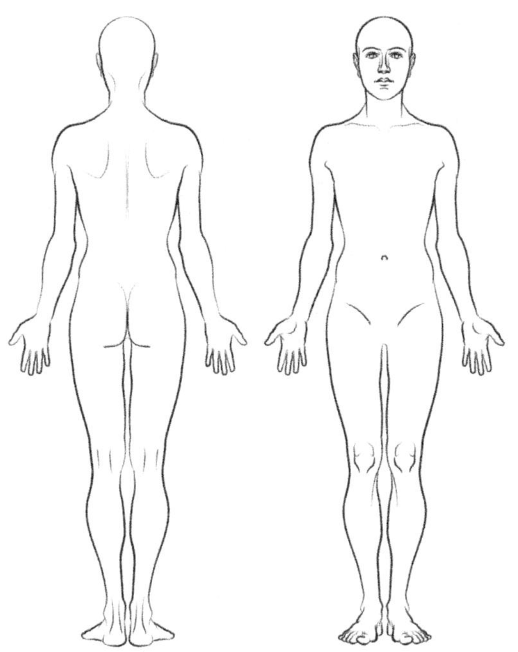

Pain Score
1 = Slight, 2 = Moderate, 3 = Severe.

	Left	Right
Jaw		
Neck		
Shoulder Girdle		
Chest		
Upper Back		
Lower Back		
Upper Arm		
Lower Arm		
Abdomen		
Hip / Buttock		
Upper Leg		
Lower Leg		

Notes

Today I Experienced			
Headache / Migraine		Diarrhoea	
Muscle Twinges / Cramps		Constipation	
Muscle Weakness		Bloating / Stomach Pain / IBS	
Skin Itching / Burning / Hives / Rash (circle all that apply)		Bladder Issues	
Bruising		Swelling	
Sweating		Stress	
Nervousness		Nausea / vomiting	
Sensitive to Sensory Stimulation (light / noise / temperature)		Numbness / Tingling (name part of body)	
Dizziness		Missed meal / unusual food	
Loss of appetite		Hormonal Changes	
Other:		Other:	
Other:		Other:	

Date: ______ ***Weather:*** ______

Hours Slept: ______ Insomnia? Yes ☐ No ☐

How did you feel on waking today? I felt refreshed: ☐

Slightly unrefreshed: ☐ Moderately unrefreshed: ☐ Severely unrefreshed: ☐

Did you exercise today? Yes ☐ No ☐ ______

		Morning	Afternoon	Evening
	3			
	2			
	1			
Fatigue	0			
	3			
	2			
	1			
Pain Levels	0			
	3			
	2			
	1			
Cognitive Symptoms / Brain Fog	0			

		Morning	Afternoon	Evening
	3			
	2			
	1			
Anxiety / Low Mood	0			
	3			
	2			
	1			
Activity Levels	0			
	3			
	2			
	1			
Other	0			

Symptom Score: 0 = No problem, 1 = Slight, 2 = Moderate, 3 = Severe. See p.3

Today's Notes:

Pain Location & Levels

Shade bodies, tick boxes or use pain score.

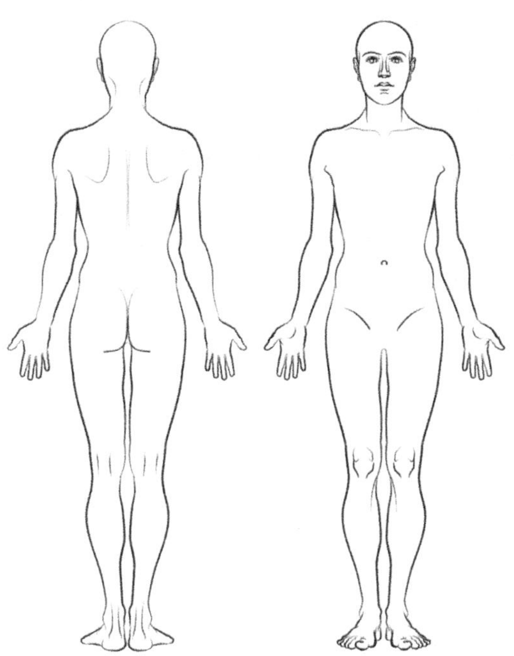

Pain Score
1 = Slight, 2 = Moderate, 3 = Severe.

	Left	Right
Jaw		
Neck		
Shoulder Girdle		
Chest		
Upper Back		
Lower Back		
Upper Arm		
Lower Arm		
Abdomen		
Hip / Buttock		
Upper Leg		
Lower Leg		

Notes

Today I Experienced			
Headache / Migraine		Diarrhoea	
Muscle Twinges / Cramps		Constipation	
Muscle Weakness		Bloating / Stomach Pain / IBS	
Skin Itching / Burning / Hives / Rash (circle all that apply)		Bladder Issues	
Bruising		Swelling	
Sweating		Stress	
Nervousness		Nausea / vomiting	
Sensitive to Sensory Stimulation (light / noise / temperature)		Numbness / Tingling (name part of body)	
Dizziness		Missed meal / unusual food	
Loss of appetite		Hormonal Changes	
Other:		Other:	
Other:		Other:	

Date: ***Weather:***

Hours Slept: Insomnia? Yes ☐ No ☐

How did you feel on waking today? I felt refreshed: ☐

Slightly unrefreshed: ☐ Moderately unrefreshed: ☐ Severely unrefreshed: ☐

Did you exercise today? Yes ☐ No ☐

		Morning	Afternoon	Evening
Fatigue	3			
	2			
	1			
	0			
Pain Levels	3			
	2			
	1			
	0			
Cognitive Symptoms / Brain Fog	3			
	2			
	1			
	0			

		Morning	Afternoon	Evening
Anxiety / Low Mood	3			
	2			
	1			
	0			
Activity Levels	3			
	2			
	1			
	0			
Other	3			
	2			
	1			
	0			

Symptom Score: 0 = No problem, 1 = Slight, 2 = Moderate, 3 = Severe. See p.3

Today's Notes:

Pain Location & Levels

Shade bodies, tick boxes or use pain score.

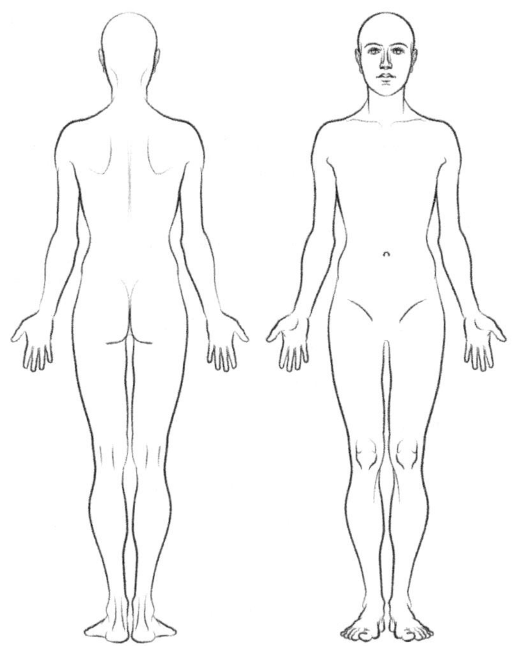

Pain Score
1 = Slight, 2 = Moderate, 3 = Severe.

	Left	Right
Jaw		
Neck		
Shoulder Girdle		
Chest		
Upper Back		
Lower Back		
Upper Arm		
Lower Arm		
Abdomen		
Hip / Buttock		
Upper Leg		
Lower Leg		

Notes

Today I Experienced			
Headache / Migraine		Diarrhoea	
Muscle Twinges / Cramps		Constipation	
Muscle Weakness		Bloating / Stomach Pain / IBS	
Skin Itching / Burning / Hives / Rash (circle all that apply)		Bladder Issues	
Bruising		Swelling	
Sweating		Stress	
Nervousness		Nausea / vomiting	
Sensitive to Sensory Stimulation (light / noise / temperature)		Numbness / Tingling (name part of body)	
Dizziness		Missed meal / unusual food	
Loss of appetite		Hormonal Changes	
Other:		Other:	
Other:		Other:	

Date: ***Weather:***

Hours Slept: Insomnia? Yes ☐ No ☐

How did you feel on waking today? I felt refreshed: ☐

Slightly unrefreshed: ☐ Moderately unrefreshed: ☐ Severely unrefreshed: ☐

Did you exercise today? Yes ☐ No ☐

		Morning	Afternoon	Evening
Fatigue	3			
	2			
	1			
	0			
Pain Levels	3			
	2			
	1			
	0			
Cognitive Symptoms / Brain Fog	3			
	2			
	1			
	0			

		Morning	Afternoon	Evening
Anxiety / Low Mood	3			
	2			
	1			
	0			
Activity Levels	3			
	2			
	1			
	0			
Other	3			
	2			
	1			
	0			

Symptom Score: 0 = No problem, 1 = Slight, 2 = Moderate, 3 = Severe. See p.3

Today's Notes:

Pain Location & Levels

Shade bodies, tick boxes or use pain score.

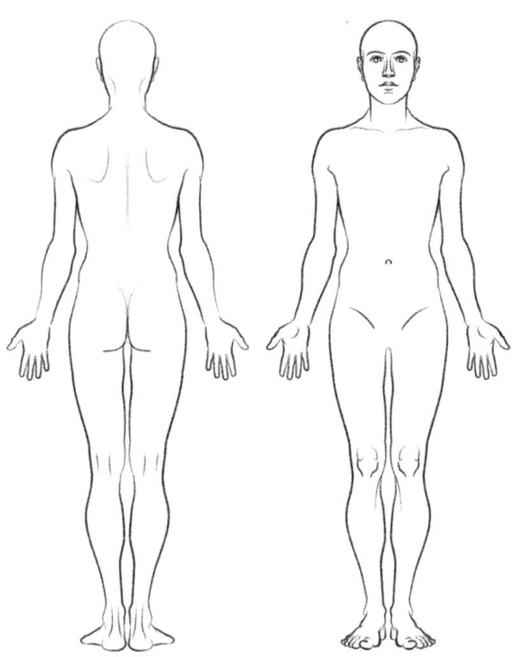

Pain Score
1 = Slight, 2 = Moderate, 3 = Severe.

	Left	Right
Jaw		
Neck		
Shoulder Girdle		
Chest		
Upper Back		
Lower Back		
Upper Arm		
Lower Arm		
Abdomen		
Hip / Buttock		
Upper Leg		
Lower Leg		

Notes

Today I Experienced			
Headache / Migraine		Diarrhoea	
Muscle Twinges / Cramps		Constipation	
Muscle Weakness		Bloating / Stomach Pain / IBS	
Skin Itching / Burning / Hives / Rash (circle all that apply)		Bladder Issues	
Bruising		Swelling	
Sweating		Stress	
Nervousness		Nausea / vomiting	
Sensitive to Sensory Stimulation (light / noise / temperature)		Numbness / Tingling (name part of body)	
Dizziness		Missed meal / unusual food	
Loss of appetite		Hormonal Changes	
Other:		Other:	
Other:		Other:	

Date: ***Weather:***

Hours Slept: Insomnia? Yes ☐ No ☐

How did you feel on waking today? I felt refreshed: ☐

Slightly unrefreshed: ☐ Moderately unrefreshed: ☐ Severely unrefreshed: ☐

Did you exercise today? Yes ☐ No ☐

		Morning	Afternoon	Evening
	3			
	2			
	1			
Fatigue	0			
	3			
	2			
	1			
Pain Levels	0			
	3			
Cognitive Symptoms / Brain Fog	2			
	1			
	0			

		Morning	Afternoon	Evening
	3			
	2			
Anxiety / Low Mood	1			
	0			
	3			
	2			
	1			
Activity Levels	0			
	3			
	2			
	1			
Other	0			

Symptom Score: 0 = No problem, 1 = Slight, 2 = Moderate, 3 = Severe. See p.3

Today's Notes:

Pain Location & Levels

Shade bodies, tick boxes or use pain score.

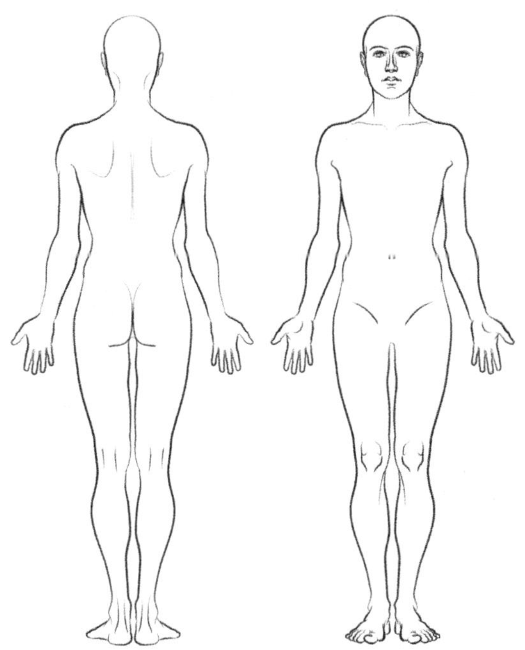

Pain Score
1 = Slight, 2 = Moderate, 3 = Severe.

	Left	Right
Jaw		
Neck		
Shoulder Girdle		
Chest		
Upper Back		
Lower Back		
Upper Arm		
Lower Arm		
Abdomen		
Hip / Buttock		
Upper Leg		
Lower Leg		

Notes

Today I Experienced			
Headache / Migraine		Diarrhoea	
Muscle Twinges / Cramps		Constipation	
Muscle Weakness		Bloating / Stomach Pain / IBS	
Skin Itching / Burning / Hives / Rash (circle all that apply)		Bladder Issues	
Bruising		Swelling	
Sweating		Stress	
Nervousness		Nausea / vomiting	
Sensitive to Sensory Stimulation (light / noise / temperature)		Numbness / Tingling (name part of body)	
Dizziness		Missed meal / unusual food	
Loss of appetite		Hormonal Changes	
Other:		Other:	
Other:		Other:	

Date: ***Weather:***

Hours Slept: Insomnia? Yes ☐ No ☐

How did you feel on waking today? I felt refreshed: ☐

Slightly unrefreshed: ☐ Moderately unrefreshed: ☐ Severely unrefreshed: ☐

Did you exercise today? Yes ☐ No ☐

		Morning	Afternoon	Evening
Fatigue	3			
	2			
	1			
	0			
Pain Levels	3			
	2			
	1			
	0			
Cognitive Symptoms / Brain Fog	3			
	2			
	1			
	0			

		Morning	Afternoon	Evening
Anxiety / Low Mood	3			
	2			
	1			
	0			
Activity Levels	3			
	2			
	1			
	0			
Other	3			
	2			
	1			
	0			

Symptom Score: 0 = No problem, 1 = Slight, 2 = Moderate, 3 = Severe. See p.3

Today's Notes:

Pain Location & Levels

Shade bodies, tick boxes or use pain score.

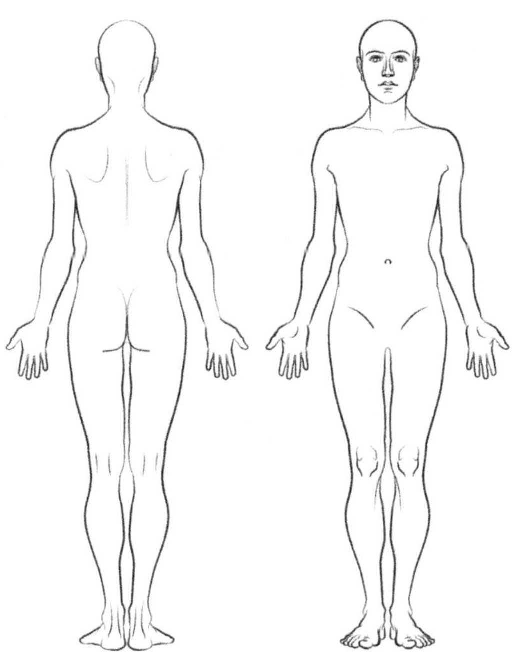

Pain Score
1 = Slight, 2 = Moderate, 3 = Severe.

	Left	Right
Jaw		
Neck		
Shoulder Girdle		
Chest		
Upper Back		
Lower Back		
Upper Arm		
Lower Arm		
Abdomen		
Hip / Buttock		
Upper Leg		
Lower Leg		

Notes

Today I Experienced			
Headache / Migraine		Diarrhoea	
Muscle Twinges / Cramps		Constipation	
Muscle Weakness		Bloating / Stomach Pain / IBS	
Skin Itching / Burning / Hives / Rash (circle all that apply)		Bladder Issues	
Bruising		Swelling	
Sweating		Stress	
Nervousness		Nausea / vomiting	
Sensitive to Sensory Stimulation (light / noise / temperature)		Numbness / Tingling (name part of body)	
Dizziness		Missed meal / unusual food	
Loss of appetite		Hormonal Changes	
Other:		Other:	
Other:		Other:	

Date: ***Weather:***

Hours Slept: Insomnia? Yes ☐ No ☐

How did you feel on waking today? I felt refreshed: ☐

Slightly unrefreshed: ☐ Moderately unrefreshed: ☐ Severely unrefreshed: ☐

Did you exercise today? Yes ☐ No ☐

		Morning	Afternoon	Evening
Fatigue	3			
	2			
	1			
	0			
Pain Levels	3			
	2			
	1			
	0			
Cognitive Symptoms / Brain Fog	3			
	2			
	1			
	0			

		Morning	Afternoon	Evening
Anxiety / Low Mood	3			
	2			
	1			
	0			
Activity Levels	3			
	2			
	1			
	0			
Other	3			
	2			
	1			
	0			

Symptom Score: 0 = No problem, 1 = Slight, 2 = Moderate, 3 = Severe. See p.3

Today's Notes:

Pain Location & Levels

Shade bodies, tick boxes or use pain score.

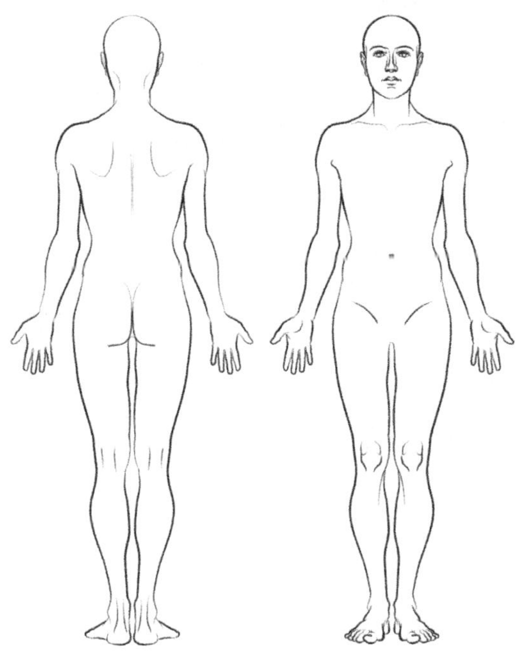

Pain Score
1 = Slight, 2 = Moderate, 3 = Severe.

	Left	Right
Jaw		
Neck		
Shoulder Girdle		
Chest		
Upper Back		
Lower Back		
Upper Arm		
Lower Arm		
Abdomen		
Hip / Buttock		
Upper Leg		
Lower Leg		

Notes

Today I Experienced			
Headache / Migraine		Diarrhoea	
Muscle Twinges / Cramps		Constipation	
Muscle Weakness		Bloating / Stomach Pain / IBS	
Skin Itching / Burning / Hives / Rash (circle all that apply)		Bladder Issues	
Bruising		Swelling	
Sweating		Stress	
Nervousness		Nausea / vomiting	
Sensitive to Sensory Stimulation (light / noise / temperature)		Numbness / Tingling (name part of body)	
Dizziness		Missed meal / unusual food	
Loss of appetite		Hormonal Changes	
Other:		Other:	
Other:		Other:	

Date: **Weather:**

Hours Slept: Insomnia? Yes ☐ No ☐

How did you feel on waking today? I felt refreshed: ☐

Slightly unrefreshed: ☐ Moderately unrefreshed: ☐ Severely unrefreshed: ☐

Did you exercise today? Yes ☐ No ☐

		Morning	Afternoon	Evening
	3			
	2			
	1			
Fatigue	0			
	3			
	2			
	1			
Pain Levels	0			
	3			
	2			
	1			
Cognitive Symptoms / Brain Fog	0			

		Morning	Afternoon	Evening
	3			
	2			
	1			
Anxiety / Low Mood	0			
	3			
	2			
	1			
Activity Levels	0			
	3			
	2			
	1			
Other	0			

Symptom Score: 0 = No problem, 1 = Slight, 2 = Moderate, 3 = Severe. See p.3

Today's Notes:

Pain Location & Levels

Shade bodies, tick boxes or use pain score.

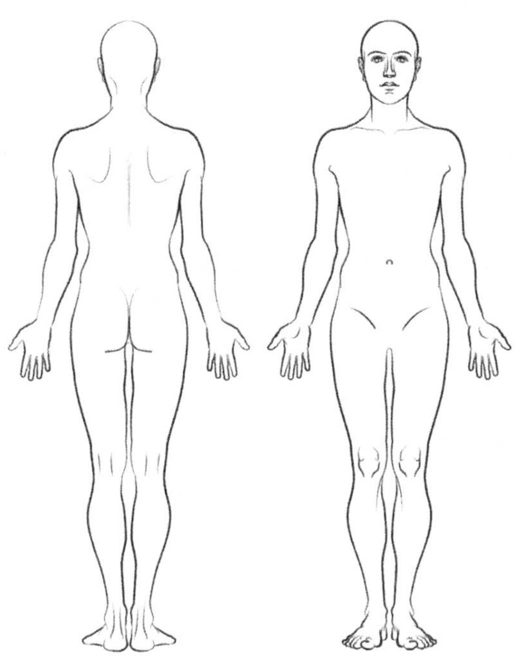

Pain Score
1 = Slight, 2 = Moderate, 3 = Severe.

	Left	Right
Jaw		
Neck		
Shoulder Girdle		
Chest		
Upper Back		
Lower Back		
Upper Arm		
Lower Arm		
Abdomen		
Hip / Buttock		
Upper Leg		
Lower Leg		

Notes

Today I Experienced			
Headache / Migraine		Diarrhoea	
Muscle Twinges / Cramps		Constipation	
Muscle Weakness		Bloating / Stomach Pain / IBS	
Skin Itching / Burning / Hives / Rash (circle all that apply)		Bladder Issues	
Bruising		Swelling	
Sweating		Stress	
Nervousness		Nausea / vomiting	
Sensitive to Sensory Stimulation (light / noise / temperature)		Numbness / Tingling (name part of body)	
Dizziness		Missed meal / unusual food	
Loss of appetite		Hormonal Changes	
Other:		Other:	
Other:		Other:	

Date: ______ ***Weather:*** ______

Hours Slept: ______ Insomnia? Yes ☐ No ☐

How did you feel on waking today? I felt refreshed: ☐

Slightly unrefreshed: ☐ Moderately unrefreshed: ☐ Severely unrefreshed: ☐

Did you exercise today? Yes ☐ No ☐ ______

		Morning	Afternoon	Evening
Fatigue	3			
	2			
	1			
	0			
Pain Levels	3			
	2			
	1			
	0			
Cognitive Symptoms / Brain Fog	3			
	2			
	1			
	0			

		Morning	Afternoon	Evening
Anxiety / Low Mood	3			
	2			
	1			
	0			
Activity Levels	3			
	2			
	1			
	0			
Other	3			
	2			
	1			
	0			

Symptom Score: 0 = No problem, 1 = Slight, 2 = Moderate, 3 = Severe. See p.3

Today's Notes:

Pain Location & Levels

Shade bodies, tick boxes or use pain score.

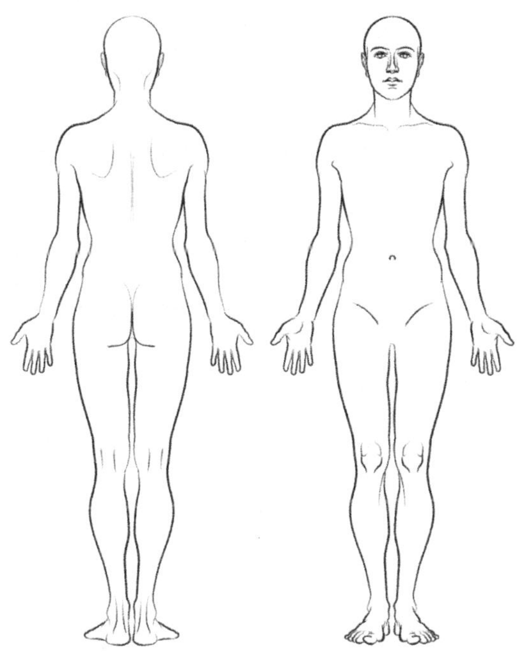

Pain Score
1 = Slight, 2 = Moderate, 3 = Severe.

	Left	Right
Jaw		
Neck		
Shoulder Girdle		
Chest		
Upper Back		
Lower Back		
Upper Arm		
Lower Arm		
Abdomen		
Hip / Buttock		
Upper Leg		
Lower Leg		

Notes

Today I Experienced			
Headache / Migraine		Diarrhoea	
Muscle Twinges / Cramps		Constipation	
Muscle Weakness		Bloating / Stomach Pain / IBS	
Skin Itching / Burning / Hives / Rash (circle all that apply)		Bladder Issues	
Bruising		Swelling	
Sweating		Stress	
Nervousness		Nausea / vomiting	
Sensitive to Sensory Stimulation (light / noise / temperature)		Numbness / Tingling (name part of body)	
Dizziness		Missed meal / unusual food	
Loss of appetite		Hormonal Changes	
Other:		Other:	
Other:		Other:	

Date: ***Weather:***

Hours Slept: Insomnia? Yes ☐ No ☐

How did you feel on waking today? I felt refreshed: ☐

Slightly unrefreshed: ☐ Moderately unrefreshed: ☐ Severely unrefreshed: ☐

Did you exercise today? Yes ☐ No ☐

		Morning	Afternoon	Evening
Fatigue	3			
	2			
	1			
	0			
Pain Levels	3			
	2			
	1			
	0			
Cognitive Symptoms / Brain Fog	3			
	2			
	1			
	0			

		Morning	Afternoon	Evening
Anxiety / Low Mood	3			
	2			
	1			
	0			
Activity Levels	3			
	2			
	1			
	0			
Other	3			
	2			
	1			
	0			

Symptom Score: 0 = No problem, 1 = Slight, 2 = Moderate, 3 = Severe. See p.3

Today's Notes:

Pain Location & Levels

Shade bodies, tick boxes or use pain score.

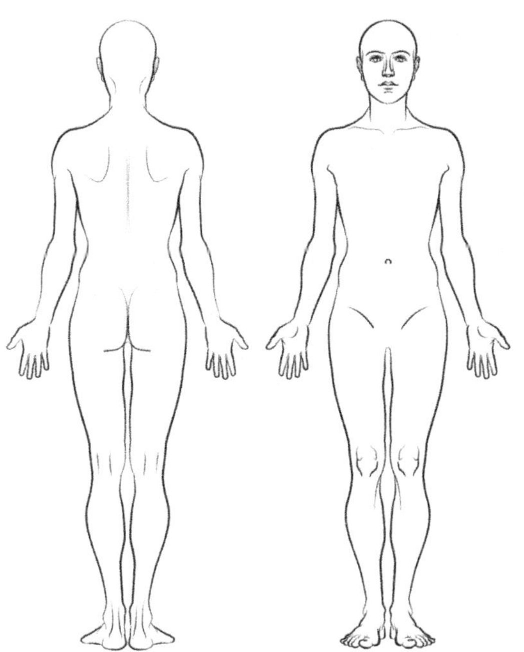

Pain Score
1 = Slight, 2 = Moderate, 3 = Severe.

	Left	Right
Jaw		
Neck		
Shoulder Girdle		
Chest		
Upper Back		
Lower Back		
Upper Arm		
Lower Arm		
Abdomen		
Hip / Buttock		
Upper Leg		
Lower Leg		

Notes

Today I Experienced			
Headache / Migraine		Diarrhoea	
Muscle Twinges / Cramps		Constipation	
Muscle Weakness		Bloating / Stomach Pain / IBS	
Skin Itching / Burning / Hives / Rash (circle all that apply)		Bladder Issues	
Bruising		Swelling	
Sweating		Stress	
Nervousness		Nausea / vomiting	
Sensitive to Sensory Stimulation (light / noise / temperature)		Numbness / Tingling (name part of body)	
Dizziness		Missed meal / unusual food	
Loss of appetite		Hormonal Changes	
Other:		Other:	
Other:		Other:	

Date: ***Weather:***

Hours Slept: Insomnia? Yes ☐ No ☐

How did you feel on waking today? I felt refreshed: ☐

Slightly unrefreshed: ☐ Moderately unrefreshed: ☐ Severely unrefreshed: ☐

Did you exercise today? Yes ☐ No ☐

		Morning	Afternoon	Evening
Fatigue	3			
	2			
	1			
	0			
Pain Levels	3			
	2			
	1			
	0			
Cognitive Symptoms / Brain Fog	3			
	2			
	1			
	0			

		Morning	Afternoon	Evening
Anxiety / Low Mood	3			
	2			
	1			
	0			
Activity Levels	3			
	2			
	1			
	0			
Other	3			
	2			
	1			
	0			

Symptom Score: 0 = No problem, 1 = Slight, 2 = Moderate, 3 = Severe. See p.3

Today's Notes:

Pain Location & Levels

Shade bodies, tick boxes or use pain score.

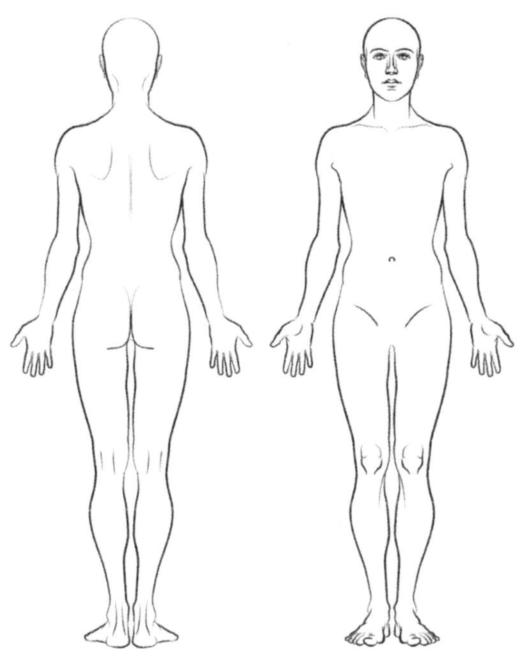

Pain Score
1 = Slight, 2 = Moderate, 3 = Severe.

	Left	Right
Jaw		
Neck		
Shoulder Girdle		
Chest		
Upper Back		
Lower Back		
Upper Arm		
Lower Arm		
Abdomen		
Hip / Buttock		
Upper Leg		
Lower Leg		

Notes

Today I Experienced			
Headache / Migraine		Diarrhoea	
Muscle Twinges / Cramps		Constipation	
Muscle Weakness		Bloating / Stomach Pain / IBS	
Skin Itching / Burning / Hives / Rash (circle all that apply)		Bladder Issues	
Bruising		Swelling	
Sweating		Stress	
Nervousness		Nausea / vomiting	
Sensitive to Sensory Stimulation (light / noise / temperature)		Numbness / Tingling (name part of body)	
Dizziness		Missed meal / unusual food	
Loss of appetite		Hormonal Changes	
Other:		Other:	
Other:		Other:	

Date: ______ ***Weather:*** ______

Hours Slept: ______ Insomnia? Yes ☐ No ☐

How did you feel on waking today? I felt refreshed: ☐

Slightly unrefreshed: ☐ Moderately unrefreshed: ☐ Severely unrefreshed: ☐

Did you exercise today? Yes ☐ No ☐ ______

		Morning	Afternoon	Evening
Fatigue	3			
	2			
	1			
	0			
Pain Levels	3			
	2			
	1			
	0			
Cognitive Symptoms / Brain Fog	3			
	2			
	1			
	0			

		Morning	Afternoon	Evening
Anxiety / Low Mood	3			
	2			
	1			
	0			
Activity Levels	3			
	2			
	1			
	0			
Other	3			
	2			
	1			
	0			

Symptom Score: 0 = No problem, 1 = Slight, 2 = Moderate, 3 = Severe. See p.3

Today's Notes:

Pain Location & Levels

Shade bodies, tick boxes or use pain score.

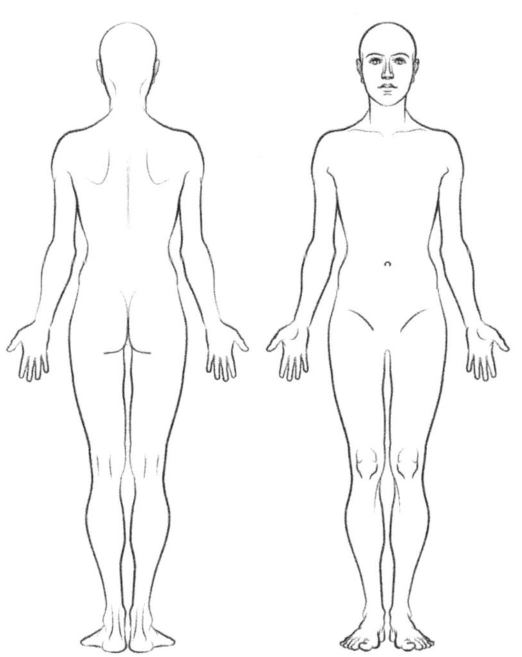

Pain Score
1 = Slight, 2 = Moderate, 3 = Severe.

	Left	Right
Jaw		
Neck		
Shoulder Girdle		
Chest		
Upper Back		
Lower Back		
Upper Arm		
Lower Arm		
Abdomen		
Hip / Buttock		
Upper Leg		
Lower Leg		

Notes

Today I Experienced			
Headache / Migraine		Diarrhoea	
Muscle Twinges / Cramps		Constipation	
Muscle Weakness		Bloating / Stomach Pain / IBS	
Skin Itching / Burning / Hives / Rash (circle all that apply)		Bladder Issues	
Bruising		Swelling	
Sweating		Stress	
Nervousness		Nausea / vomiting	
Sensitive to Sensory Stimulation (light / noise / temperature)		Numbness / Tingling (name part of body)	
Dizziness		Missed meal / unusual food	
Loss of appetite		Hormonal Changes	
Other:		Other:	
Other:		Other:	

Date: ***Weather:***

Hours Slept: Insomnia? Yes ☐ No ☐

How did you feel on waking today? I felt refreshed: ☐

Slightly unrefreshed: ☐ Moderately unrefreshed: ☐ Severely unrefreshed: ☐

Did you exercise today? Yes ☐ No ☐

		Morning	Afternoon	Evening
	3			
	2			
	1			
Fatigue	0			
	3			
	2			
	1			
Pain Levels	0			
	3			
	2			
	1			
Cognitive Symptoms / Brain Fog	0			

		Morning	Afternoon	Evening
	3			
	2			
	1			
Anxiety / Low Mood	0			
	3			
	2			
	1			
Activity Levels	0			
	3			
	2			
	1			
Other	0			

Symptom Score: 0 = No problem, 1 = Slight, 2 = Moderate, 3 = Severe. See p.3

Today's Notes:

Pain Location & Levels

Shade bodies, tick boxes or use pain score.

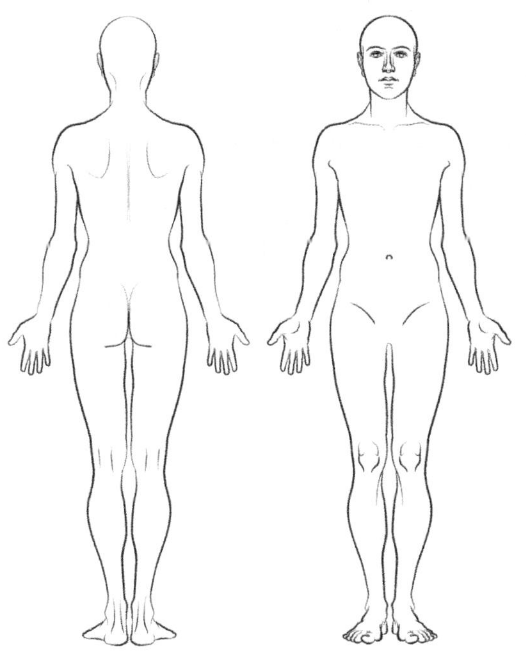

Pain Score
1 = Slight, 2 = Moderate, 3 = Severe.

	Left	Right
Jaw		
Neck		
Shoulder Girdle		
Chest		
Upper Back		
Lower Back		
Upper Arm		
Lower Arm		
Abdomen		
Hip / Buttock		
Upper Leg		
Lower Leg		

Notes

Today I Experienced			
Headache / Migraine		Diarrhoea	
Muscle Twinges / Cramps		Constipation	
Muscle Weakness		Bloating / Stomach Pain / IBS	
Skin Itching / Burning / Hives / Rash (circle all that apply)		Bladder Issues	
Bruising		Swelling	
Sweating		Stress	
Nervousness		Nausea / vomiting	
Sensitive to Sensory Stimulation (light / noise / temperature)		Numbness / Tingling (name part of body)	
Dizziness		Missed meal / unusual food	
Loss of appetite		Hormonal Changes	
Other:		Other:	
Other:		Other:	

Date: ***Weather:***

Hours Slept: Insomnia? Yes ☐ No ☐

How did you feel on waking today? I felt refreshed: ☐

Slightly unrefreshed: ☐ Moderately unrefreshed: ☐ Severely unrefreshed: ☐

Did you exercise today? Yes ☐ No ☐

		Morning	Afternoon	Evening
Fatigue	3			
	2			
	1			
	0			
Pain Levels	3			
	2			
	1			
	0			
Cognitive Symptoms / Brain Fog	3			
	2			
	1			
	0			

		Morning	Afternoon	Evening
Anxiety / Low Mood	3			
	2			
	1			
	0			
Activity Levels	3			
	2			
	1			
	0			
Other	3			
	2			
	1			
	0			

Symptom Score: 0 = No problem, 1 = Slight, 2 = Moderate, 3 = Severe. See p.3

Today's Notes:

Pain Location & Levels

Shade bodies, tick boxes or use pain score.

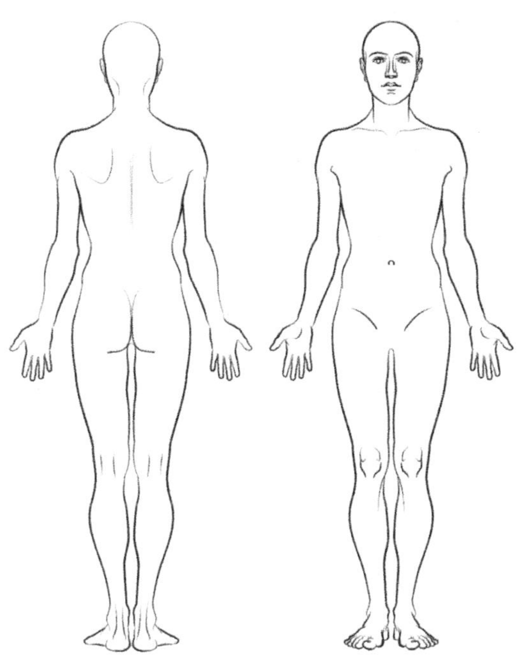

Pain Score
1 = Slight, 2 = Moderate, 3 = Severe.

	Left	Right
Jaw		
Neck		
Shoulder Girdle		
Chest		
Upper Back		
Lower Back		
Upper Arm		
Lower Arm		
Abdomen		
Hip / Buttock		
Upper Leg		
Lower Leg		

Notes

Today I Experienced			
Headache / Migraine		Diarrhoea	
Muscle Twinges / Cramps		Constipation	
Muscle Weakness		Bloating / Stomach Pain / IBS	
Skin Itching / Burning / Hives / Rash (circle all that apply)		Bladder Issues	
Bruising		Swelling	
Sweating		Stress	
Nervousness		Nausea / vomiting	
Sensitive to Sensory Stimulation (light / noise / temperature)		Numbness / Tingling (name part of body)	
Dizziness		Missed meal / unusual food	
Loss of appetite		Hormonal Changes	
Other:		Other:	
Other:		Other:	

Date: ***Weather:***

Hours Slept: Insomnia? Yes ☐ No ☐

How did you feel on waking today? I felt refreshed: ☐

Slightly unrefreshed: ☐ Moderately unrefreshed: ☐ Severely unrefreshed: ☐

Did you exercise today? Yes ☐ No ☐

		Morning	Afternoon	Evening
Fatigue	3			
	2			
	1			
	0			
Pain Levels	3			
	2			
	1			
	0			
Cognitive Symptoms / Brain Fog	3			
	2			
	1			
	0			

		Morning	Afternoon	Evening
Anxiety / Low Mood	3			
	2			
	1			
	0			
Activity Levels	3			
	2			
	1			
	0			
Other	3			
	2			
	1			
	0			

Symptom Score: 0 = No problem, 1 = Slight, 2 = Moderate, 3 = Severe. See p.3

Today's Notes:

Pain Location & Levels

Shade bodies, tick boxes or use pain score.

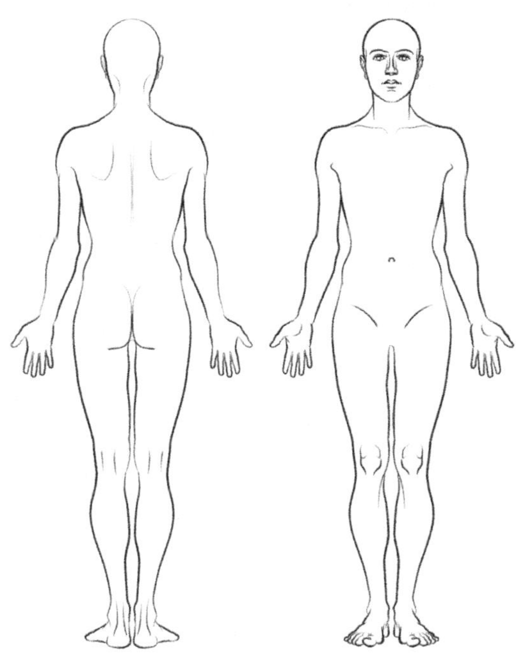

Pain Score
1 = Slight, 2 = Moderate, 3 = Severe.

	Left	Right
Jaw		
Neck		
Shoulder Girdle		
Chest		
Upper Back		
Lower Back		
Upper Arm		
Lower Arm		
Abdomen		
Hip / Buttock		
Upper Leg		
Lower Leg		

Notes

Today I Experienced			
Headache / Migraine		Diarrhoea	
Muscle Twinges / Cramps		Constipation	
Muscle Weakness		Bloating / Stomach Pain / IBS	
Skin Itching / Burning / Hives / Rash (circle all that apply)		Bladder Issues	
Bruising		Swelling	
Sweating		Stress	
Nervousness		Nausea / vomiting	
Sensitive to Sensory Stimulation (light / noise / temperature)		Numbness / Tingling (name part of body)	
Dizziness		Missed meal / unusual food	
Loss of appetite		Hormonal Changes	
Other:		Other:	
Other:		Other:	

Date: ***Weather:***

Hours Slept: Insomnia? Yes ☐ No ☐

How did you feel on waking today? I felt refreshed: ☐

Slightly unrefreshed: ☐ Moderately unrefreshed: ☐ Severely unrefreshed: ☐

Did you exercise today? Yes ☐ No ☐

		Morning	Afternoon	Evening
Fatigue	3			
	2			
	1			
	0			
Pain Levels	3			
	2			
	1			
	0			
Cognitive Symptoms / Brain Fog	3			
	2			
	1			
	0			

		Morning	Afternoon	Evening
Anxiety / Low Mood	3			
	2			
	1			
	0			
Activity Levels	3			
	2			
	1			
	0			
Other	3			
	2			
	1			
	0			

Symptom Score: 0 = No problem, 1 = Slight, 2 = Moderate, 3 = Severe. See p.3

Today's Notes:

Pain Location & Levels

Shade bodies, tick boxes or use pain score.

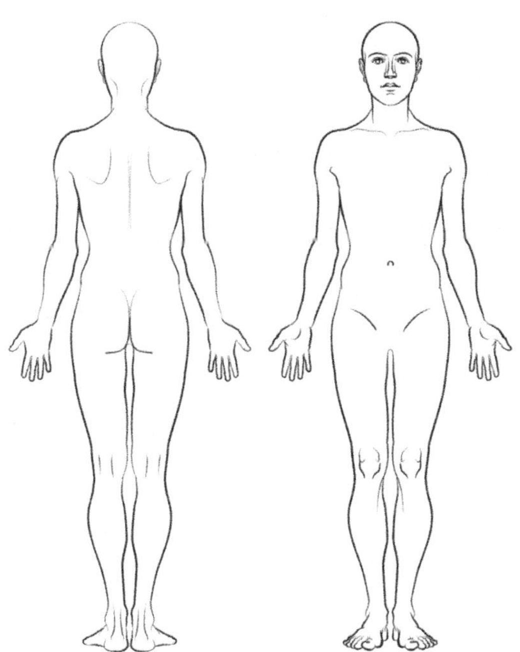

Pain Score
1 = Slight, 2 = Moderate, 3 = Severe.

	Left	Right
Jaw		
Neck		
Shoulder Girdle		
Chest		
Upper Back		
Lower Back		
Upper Arm		
Lower Arm		
Abdomen		
Hip / Buttock		
Upper Leg		
Lower Leg		

Notes

Today I Experienced			
Headache / Migraine		Diarrhoea	
Muscle Twinges / Cramps		Constipation	
Muscle Weakness		Bloating / Stomach Pain / IBS	
Skin Itching / Burning / Hives / Rash (circle all that apply)		Bladder Issues	
Bruising		Swelling	
Sweating		Stress	
Nervousness		Nausea / vomiting	
Sensitive to Sensory Stimulation (light / noise / temperature)		Numbness / Tingling (name part of body)	
Dizziness		Missed meal / unusual food	
Loss of appetite		Hormonal Changes	
Other:		Other:	
Other:		Other:	

Date: ***Weather:***

Hours Slept: Insomnia? Yes ☐ No ☐

How did you feel on waking today? I felt refreshed: ☐

Slightly unrefreshed: ☐ Moderately unrefreshed: ☐ Severely unrefreshed: ☐

Did you exercise today? Yes ☐ No ☐

		Morning	Afternoon	Evening
Fatigue	3			
	2			
	1			
	0			
Pain Levels	3			
	2			
	1			
	0			
Cognitive Symptoms / Brain Fog	3			
	2			
	1			
	0			

		Morning	Afternoon	Evening
Anxiety / Low Mood	3			
	2			
	1			
	0			
Activity Levels	3			
	2			
	1			
	0			
Other	3			
	2			
	1			
	0			

Symptom Score: 0 = No problem, 1 = Slight, 2 = Moderate, 3 = Severe. See p.3

Today's Notes:

Pain Location & Levels

Shade bodies, tick boxes or use pain score.

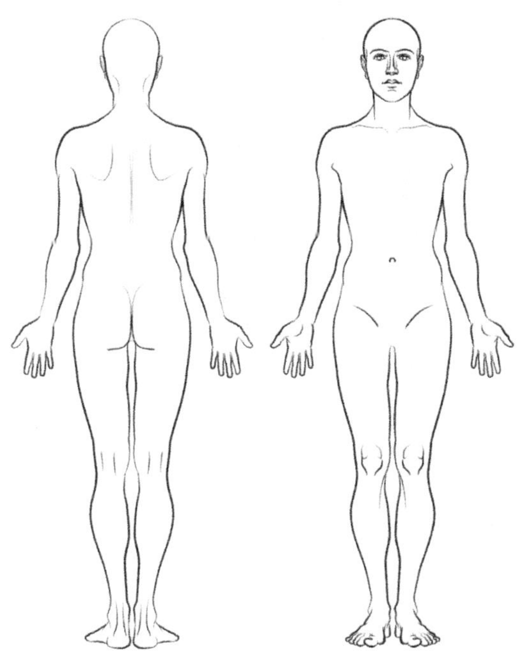

Pain Score
1 = Slight, 2 = Moderate, 3 = Severe.

	Left	Right
Jaw		
Neck		
Shoulder Girdle		
Chest		
Upper Back		
Lower Back		
Upper Arm		
Lower Arm		
Abdomen		
Hip / Buttock		
Upper Leg		
Lower Leg		

Notes

Today I Experienced			
Headache / Migraine		Diarrhoea	
Muscle Twinges / Cramps		Constipation	
Muscle Weakness		Bloating / Stomach Pain / IBS	
Skin Itching / Burning / Hives / Rash (circle all that apply)		Bladder Issues	
Bruising		Swelling	
Sweating		Stress	
Nervousness		Nausea / vomiting	
Sensitive to Sensory Stimulation (light / noise / temperature)		Numbness / Tingling (name part of body)	
Dizziness		Missed meal / unusual food	
Loss of appetite		Hormonal Changes	
Other:		Other:	
Other:		Other:	

Date: ***Weather:***

Hours Slept: Insomnia? Yes ☐ No ☐

How did you feel on waking today? I felt refreshed: ☐

Slightly unrefreshed: ☐ Moderately unrefreshed: ☐ Severely unrefreshed: ☐

Did you exercise today? Yes ☐ No ☐

		Morning	Afternoon	Evening
Fatigue	3			
	2			
	1			
	0			
Pain Levels	3			
	2			
	1			
	0			
Cognitive Symptoms / Brain Fog	3			
	2			
	1			
	0			

		Morning	Afternoon	Evening
Anxiety / Low Mood	3			
	2			
	1			
	0			
Activity Levels	3			
	2			
	1			
	0			
Other	3			
	2			
	1			
	0			

Symptom Score: 0 = No problem, 1 = Slight, 2 = Moderate, 3 = Severe. See p.3

Today's Notes:

Pain Location & Levels

Shade bodies, tick boxes or use pain score.

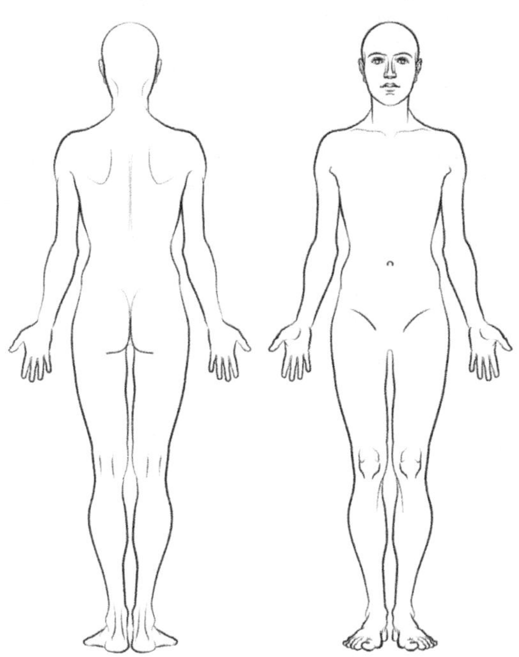

Pain Score
1 = Slight, 2 = Moderate, 3 = Severe.

	Left	Right
Jaw		
Neck		
Shoulder Girdle		
Chest		
Upper Back		
Lower Back		
Upper Arm		
Lower Arm		
Abdomen		
Hip / Buttock		
Upper Leg		
Lower Leg		

Notes

Today I Experienced			
Headache / Migraine		Diarrhoea	
Muscle Twinges / Cramps		Constipation	
Muscle Weakness		Bloating / Stomach Pain / IBS	
Skin Itching / Burning / Hives / Rash (circle all that apply)		Bladder Issues	
Bruising		Swelling	
Sweating		Stress	
Nervousness		Nausea / vomiting	
Sensitive to Sensory Stimulation (light / noise / temperature)		Numbness / Tingling (name part of body)	
Dizziness		Missed meal / unusual food	
Loss of appetite		Hormonal Changes	
Other:		Other:	
Other:		Other:	

Date: ***Weather:***

Hours Slept: Insomnia? Yes ☐ No ☐

How did you feel on waking today? I felt refreshed: ☐

Slightly unrefreshed: ☐ Moderately unrefreshed: ☐ Severely unrefreshed: ☐

Did you exercise today? Yes ☐ No ☐

		Morning	Afternoon	Evening
Fatigue	3			
	2			
	1			
	0			
Pain Levels	3			
	2			
	1			
	0			
Cognitive Symptoms / Brain Fog	3			
	2			
	1			
	0			

		Morning	Afternoon	Evening
Anxiety / Low Mood	3			
	2			
	1			
	0			
Activity Levels	3			
	2			
	1			
	0			
Other	3			
	2			
	1			
	0			

Symptom Score: 0 = No problem, 1 = Slight, 2 = Moderate, 3 = Severe. See p.3

Today's Notes:

Pain Location & Levels

Shade bodies, tick boxes or use pain score.

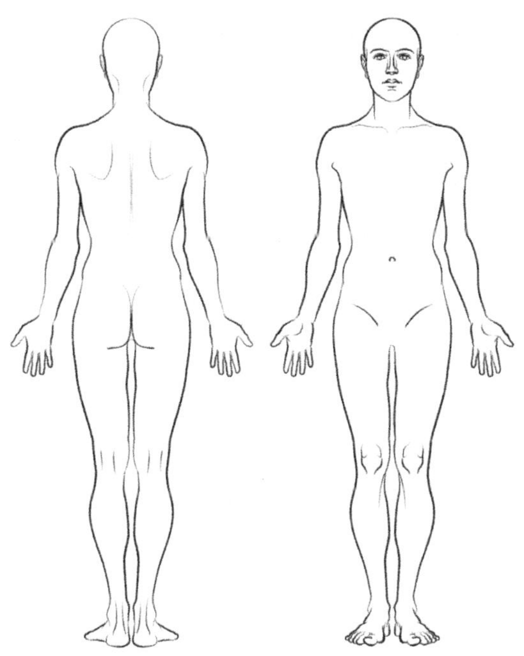

Pain Score
1 = Slight, 2 = Moderate, 3 = Severe.

	Left	Right
Jaw		
Neck		
Shoulder Girdle		
Chest		
Upper Back		
Lower Back		
Upper Arm		
Lower Arm		
Abdomen		
Hip / Buttock		
Upper Leg		
Lower Leg		

Notes

Today I Experienced			
Headache / Migraine		Diarrhoea	
Muscle Twinges / Cramps		Constipation	
Muscle Weakness		Bloating / Stomach Pain / IBS	
Skin Itching / Burning / Hives / Rash (circle all that apply)		Bladder Issues	
Bruising		Swelling	
Sweating		Stress	
Nervousness		Nausea / vomiting	
Sensitive to Sensory Stimulation (light / noise / temperature)		Numbness / Tingling (name part of body)	
Dizziness		Missed meal / unusual food	
Loss of appetite		Hormonal Changes	
Other:		Other:	
Other:		Other:	

Date: ***Weather:***

Hours Slept: Insomnia? Yes ☐ No ☐

How did you feel on waking today? I felt refreshed: ☐

Slightly unrefreshed: ☐ Moderately unrefreshed: ☐ Severely unrefreshed: ☐

Did you exercise today? Yes ☐ No ☐

		Morning	Afternoon	Evening
Fatigue	3			
	2			
	1			
	0			
Pain Levels	3			
	2			
	1			
	0			
Cognitive Symptoms / Brain Fog	3			
	2			
	1			
	0			

		Morning	Afternoon	Evening
Anxiety / Low Mood	3			
	2			
	1			
	0			
Activity Levels	3			
	2			
	1			
	0			
Other	3			
	2			
	1			
	0			

Symptom Score: 0 = No problem, 1 = Slight, 2 = Moderate, 3 = Severe. See p.3

Today's Notes:

Pain Location & Levels

Shade bodies, tick boxes or use pain score.

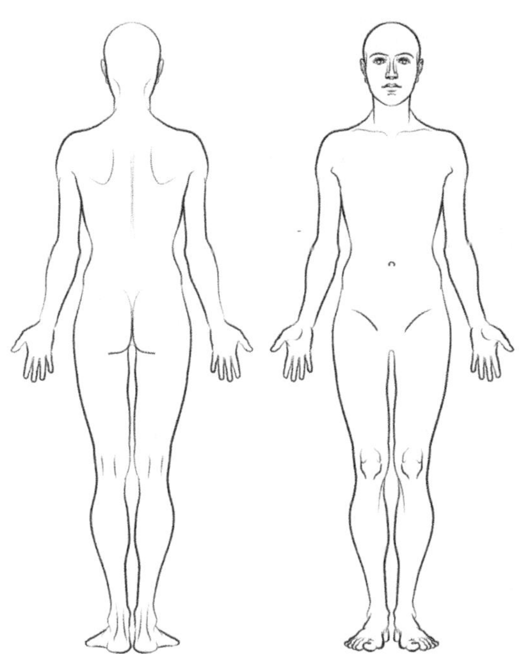

Pain Score
1 = Slight, 2 = Moderate, 3 = Severe.

	Left	Right
Jaw		
Neck		
Shoulder Girdle		
Chest		
Upper Back		
Lower Back		
Upper Arm		
Lower Arm		
Abdomen		
Hip / Buttock		
Upper Leg		
Lower Leg		

Notes

Today I Experienced			
Headache / Migraine		Diarrhoea	
Muscle Twinges / Cramps		Constipation	
Muscle Weakness		Bloating / Stomach Pain / IBS	
Skin Itching / Burning / Hives / Rash (circle all that apply)		Bladder Issues	
Bruising		Swelling	
Sweating		Stress	
Nervousness		Nausea / vomiting	
Sensitive to Sensory Stimulation (light / noise / temperature)		Numbness / Tingling (name part of body)	
Dizziness		Missed meal / unusual food	
Loss of appetite		Hormonal Changes	
Other:		Other:	
Other:		Other:	

Date: ***Weather:***

Hours Slept: Insomnia? Yes ☐ No ☐

How did you feel on waking today? I felt refreshed: ☐

Slightly unrefreshed: ☐ Moderately unrefreshed: ☐ Severely unrefreshed: ☐

Did you exercise today? Yes ☐ No ☐

		Morning	Afternoon	Evening
	3			
	2			
	1			
Fatigue	0			
	3			
	2			
	1			
Pain Levels	0			
	3			
	2			
	1			
Cognitive Symptoms / Brain Fog	0			

		Morning	Afternoon	Evening
	3			
	2			
	1			
Anxiety / Low Mood	0			
	3			
	2			
	1			
Activity Levels	0			
	3			
	2			
	1			
Other	0			

Symptom Score: 0 = No problem, 1 = Slight, 2 = Moderate, 3 = Severe. See p.3

Today's Notes:

Pain Location & Levels

Shade bodies, tick boxes or use pain score.

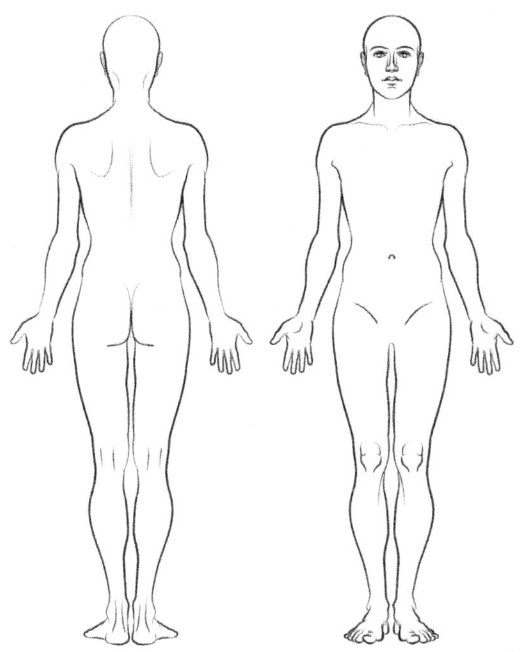

Pain Score
1 = Slight, 2 = Moderate, 3 = Severe.

	Left	Right
Jaw		
Neck		
Shoulder Girdle		
Chest		
Upper Back		
Lower Back		
Upper Arm		
Lower Arm		
Abdomen		
Hip / Buttock		
Upper Leg		
Lower Leg		

Notes

Today I Experienced			
Headache / Migraine		Diarrhoea	
Muscle Twinges / Cramps		Constipation	
Muscle Weakness		Bloating / Stomach Pain / IBS	
Skin Itching / Burning / Hives / Rash (circle all that apply)		Bladder Issues	
Bruising		Swelling	
Sweating		Stress	
Nervousness		Nausea / vomiting	
Sensitive to Sensory Stimulation (light / noise / temperature)		Numbness / Tingling (name part of body)	
Dizziness		Missed meal / unusual food	
Loss of appetite		Hormonal Changes	
Other:		Other:	
Other:		Other:	

Date: ***Weather:***

Hours Slept: Insomnia? Yes ☐ No ☐

How did you feel on waking today? I felt refreshed: ☐

Slightly unrefreshed: ☐ Moderately unrefreshed: ☐ Severely unrefreshed: ☐

Did you exercise today? Yes ☐ No ☐

		Morning	Afternoon	Evening
	3			
	2			
	1			
Fatigue	0			
	3			
	2			
	1			
Pain Levels	0			
	3			
	2			
	1			
Cognitive Symptoms / Brain Fog	0			

		Morning	Afternoon	Evening
	3			
	2			
	1			
Anxiety / Low Mood	0			
	3			
	2			
	1			
Activity Levels	0			
	3			
	2			
	1			
Other	0			

Symptom Score: 0 = No problem, 1 = Slight, 2 = Moderate, 3 = Severe. See p.3

Today's Notes:

Pain Location & Levels

Shade bodies, tick boxes or use pain score.

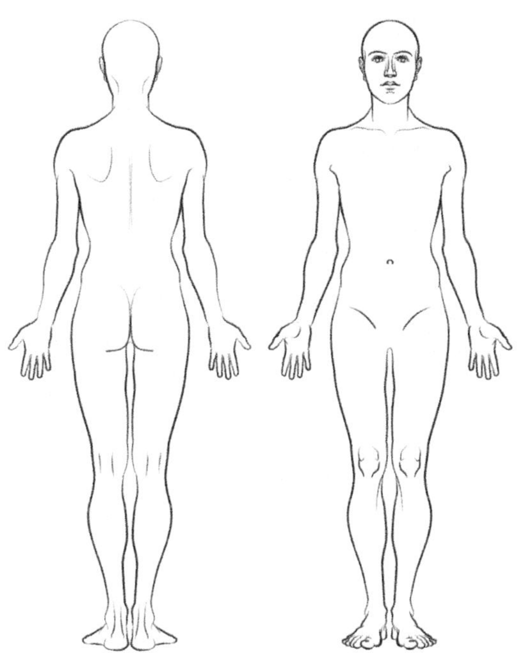

Pain Score
1 = Slight, 2 = Moderate, 3 = Severe.

	Left	Right
Jaw		
Neck		
Shoulder Girdle		
Chest		
Upper Back		
Lower Back		
Upper Arm		
Lower Arm		
Abdomen		
Hip / Buttock		
Upper Leg		
Lower Leg		

Notes

Today I Experienced			
Headache / Migraine		Diarrhoea	
Muscle Twinges / Cramps		Constipation	
Muscle Weakness		Bloating / Stomach Pain / IBS	
Skin Itching / Burning / Hives / Rash (circle all that apply)		Bladder Issues	
Bruising		Swelling	
Sweating		Stress	
Nervousness		Nausea / vomiting	
Sensitive to Sensory Stimulation (light / noise / temperature)		Numbness / Tingling (name part of body)	
Dizziness		Missed meal / unusual food	
Loss of appetite		Hormonal Changes	
Other:		Other:	
Other:		Other:	

Date: ***Weather:***

Hours Slept: Insomnia? Yes ☐ No ☐

How did you feel on waking today? I felt refreshed: ☐

Slightly unrefreshed: ☐ Moderately unrefreshed: ☐ Severely unrefreshed: ☐

Did you exercise today? Yes ☐ No ☐

		Morning	Afternoon	Evening
Fatigue	3			
	2			
	1			
	0			
Pain Levels	3			
	2			
	1			
	0			
Cognitive Symptoms / Brain Fog	3			
	2			
	1			
	0			

		Morning	Afternoon	Evening
Anxiety / Low Mood	3			
	2			
	1			
	0			
Activity Levels	3			
	2			
	1			
	0			
Other	3			
	2			
	1			
	0			

Symptom Score: 0 = No problem, 1 = Slight, 2 = Moderate, 3 = Severe. See p.3

Today's Notes:

Pain Location & Levels

Shade bodies, tick boxes or use pain score.

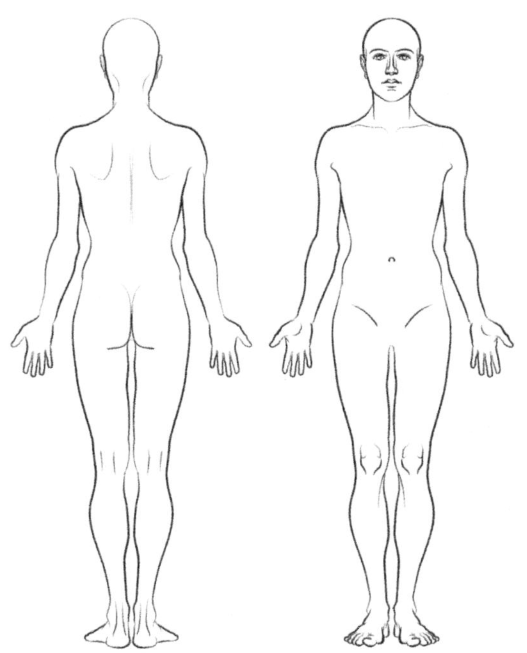

Pain Score
1 = Slight, 2 = Moderate, 3 = Severe.

	Left	Right
Jaw		
Neck		
Shoulder Girdle		
Chest		
Upper Back		
Lower Back		
Upper Arm		
Lower Arm		
Abdomen		
Hip / Buttock		
Upper Leg		
Lower Leg		

Notes

Today I Experienced			
Headache / Migraine		Diarrhoea	
Muscle Twinges / Cramps		Constipation	
Muscle Weakness		Bloating / Stomach Pain / IBS	
Skin Itching / Burning / Hives / Rash (circle all that apply)		Bladder Issues	
Bruising		Swelling	
Sweating		Stress	
Nervousness		Nausea / vomiting	
Sensitive to Sensory Stimulation (light / noise / temperature)		Numbness / Tingling (name part of body)	
Dizziness		Missed meal / unusual food	
Loss of appetite		Hormonal Changes	
Other:		Other:	
Other:		Other:	

Date: ***Weather:***

Hours Slept: Insomnia? Yes ☐ No ☐

How did you feel on waking today? I felt refreshed: ☐

Slightly unrefreshed: ☐ Moderately unrefreshed: ☐ Severely unrefreshed: ☐

Did you exercise today? Yes ☐ No ☐

		Morning	Afternoon	Evening
	3			
	2			
	1			
Fatigue	0			
	3			
	2			
	1			
Pain Levels	0			
	3			
	2			
	1			
Cognitive Symptoms / Brain Fog	0			

		Morning	Afternoon	Evening
	3			
	2			
	1			
Anxiety / Low Mood	0			
	3			
	2			
	1			
Activity Levels	0			
	3			
	2			
	1			
Other	0			

Symptom Score: 0 = No problem, 1 = Slight, 2 = Moderate, 3 = Severe. See p.3

Today's Notes:

Pain Location & Levels

Shade bodies, tick boxes or use pain score.

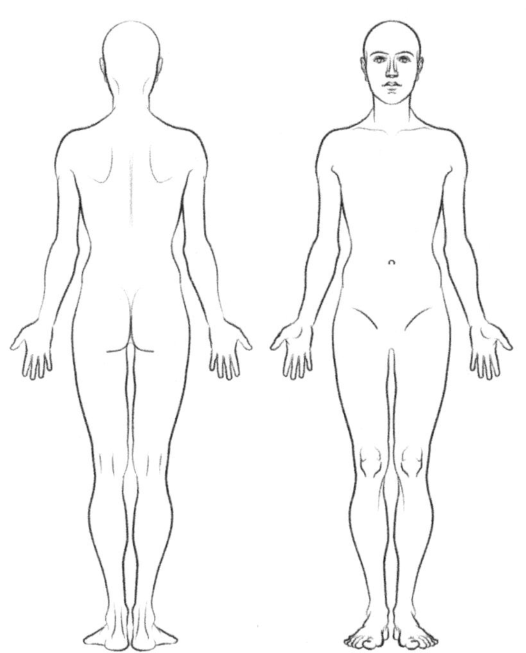

Pain Score
1 = Slight, 2 = Moderate, 3 = Severe.

	Left	Right
Jaw		
Neck		
Shoulder Girdle		
Chest		
Upper Back		
Lower Back		
Upper Arm		
Lower Arm		
Abdomen		
Hip / Buttock		
Upper Leg		
Lower Leg		

Notes

Today I Experienced			
Headache / Migraine		Diarrhoea	
Muscle Twinges / Cramps		Constipation	
Muscle Weakness		Bloating / Stomach Pain / IBS	
Skin Itching / Burning / Hives / Rash (circle all that apply)		Bladder Issues	
Bruising		Swelling	
Sweating		Stress	
Nervousness		Nausea / vomiting	
Sensitive to Sensory Stimulation (light / noise / temperature)		Numbness / Tingling (name part of body)	
Dizziness		Missed meal / unusual food	
Loss of appetite		Hormonal Changes	
Other:		Other:	
Other:		Other:	

Date: ______ ***Weather:*** ______

Hours Slept: ______ Insomnia? Yes ☐ No ☐

How did you feel on waking today? I felt refreshed: ☐

Slightly unrefreshed: ☐ Moderately unrefreshed: ☐ Severely unrefreshed: ☐

Did you exercise today? Yes ☐ No ☐ ______

		Morning	Afternoon	Evening
	3			
	2			
	1			
Fatigue	0			
	3			
	2			
	1			
Pain Levels	0			
	3			
	2			
	1			
Cognitive Symptoms / Brain Fog	0			

		Morning	Afternoon	Evening
	3			
	2			
	1			
Anxiety / Low Mood	0			
	3			
	2			
	1			
Activity Levels	0			
	3			
	2			
	1			
Other	0			

Symptom Score: 0 = No problem, 1 = Slight, 2 = Moderate, 3 = Severe. See p.3

Today's Notes:

Pain Location & Levels

Shade bodies, tick boxes or use pain score.

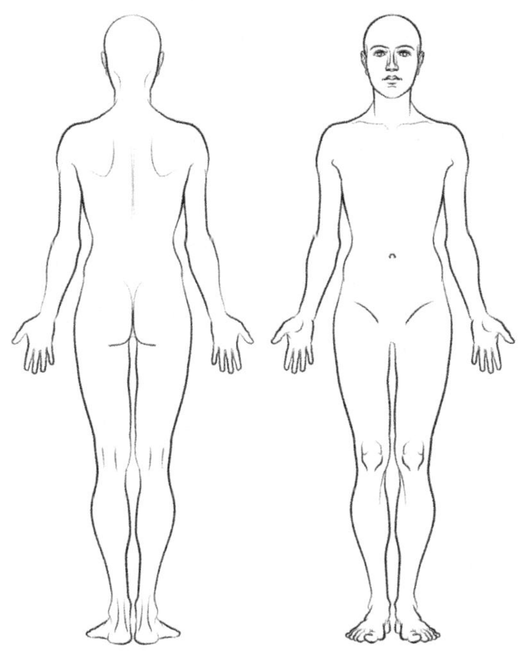

Pain Score
1 = Slight, 2 = Moderate, 3 = Severe.

	Left	Right
Jaw		
Neck		
Shoulder Girdle		
Chest		
Upper Back		
Lower Back		
Upper Arm		
Lower Arm		
Abdomen		
Hip / Buttock		
Upper Leg		
Lower Leg		

Notes

Today I Experienced			
Headache / Migraine		Diarrhoea	
Muscle Twinges / Cramps		Constipation	
Muscle Weakness		Bloating / Stomach Pain / IBS	
Skin Itching / Burning / Hives / Rash (circle all that apply)		Bladder Issues	
Bruising		Swelling	
Sweating		Stress	
Nervousness		Nausea / vomiting	
Sensitive to Sensory Stimulation (light / noise / temperature)		Numbness / Tingling (name part of body)	
Dizziness		Missed meal / unusual food	
Loss of appetite		Hormonal Changes	
Other:		Other:	
Other:		Other:	

Date: ***Weather:***

Hours Slept: Insomnia? Yes ☐ No ☐

How did you feel on waking today? I felt refreshed: ☐

Slightly unrefreshed: ☐ Moderately unrefreshed: ☐ Severely unrefreshed: ☐

Did you exercise today? Yes ☐ No ☐

		Morning	Afternoon	Evening
Fatigue	3			
	2			
	1			
	0			
Pain Levels	3			
	2			
	1			
	0			
Cognitive Symptoms / Brain Fog	3			
	2			
	1			
	0			

		Morning	Afternoon	Evening
Anxiety / Low Mood	3			
	2			
	1			
	0			
Activity Levels	3			
	2			
	1			
	0			
Other	3			
	2			
	1			
	0			

Symptom Score: 0 = No problem, 1 = Slight, 2 = Moderate, 3 = Severe. See p.3

Today's Notes:

Pain Location & Levels

Shade bodies, tick boxes or use pain score.

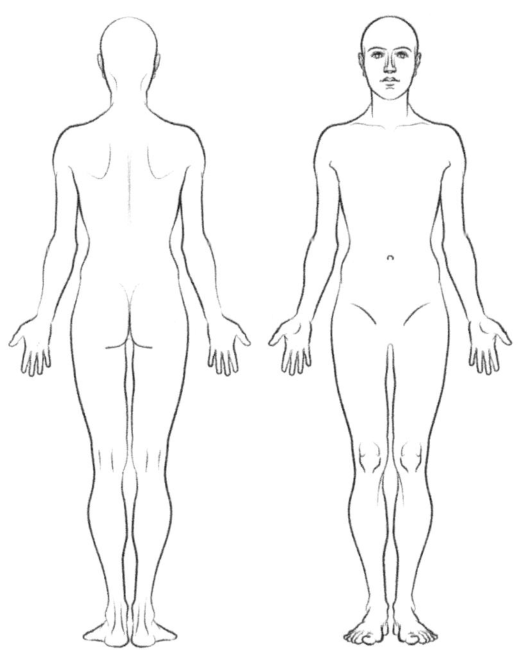

Pain Score
1 = Slight, 2 = Moderate, 3 = Severe.

	Left	Right
Jaw		
Neck		
Shoulder Girdle		
Chest		
Upper Back		
Lower Back		
Upper Arm		
Lower Arm		
Abdomen		
Hip / Buttock		
Upper Leg		
Lower Leg		

Notes

Today I Experienced			
Headache / Migraine		Diarrhoea	
Muscle Twinges / Cramps		Constipation	
Muscle Weakness		Bloating / Stomach Pain / IBS	
Skin Itching / Burning / Hives / Rash (circle all that apply)		Bladder Issues	
Bruising		Swelling	
Sweating		Stress	
Nervousness		Nausea / vomiting	
Sensitive to Sensory Stimulation (light / noise / temperature)		Numbness / Tingling (name part of body)	
Dizziness		Missed meal / unusual food	
Loss of appetite		Hormonal Changes	
Other:		Other:	
Other:		Other:	

Date: ***Weather:***

Hours Slept: Insomnia? Yes ☐ No ☐

How did you feel on waking today? I felt refreshed: ☐

Slightly unrefreshed: ☐ Moderately unrefreshed: ☐ Severely unrefreshed: ☐

Did you exercise today? Yes ☐ No ☐

		Morning	Afternoon	Evening
	3			
	2			
	1			
Fatigue	0			
	3			
	2			
	1			
Pain Levels	0			
	3			
	2			
	1			
Cognitive Symptoms / Brain Fog	0			

		Morning	Afternoon	Evening
	3			
	2			
	1			
Anxiety / Low Mood	0			
	3			
	2			
	1			
Activity Levels	0			
	3			
	2			
	1			
Other	0			

Symptom Score: 0 = No problem, 1 = Slight, 2 = Moderate, 3 = Severe. See p.3

Today's Notes:

Pain Location & Levels

Shade bodies, tick boxes or use pain score.

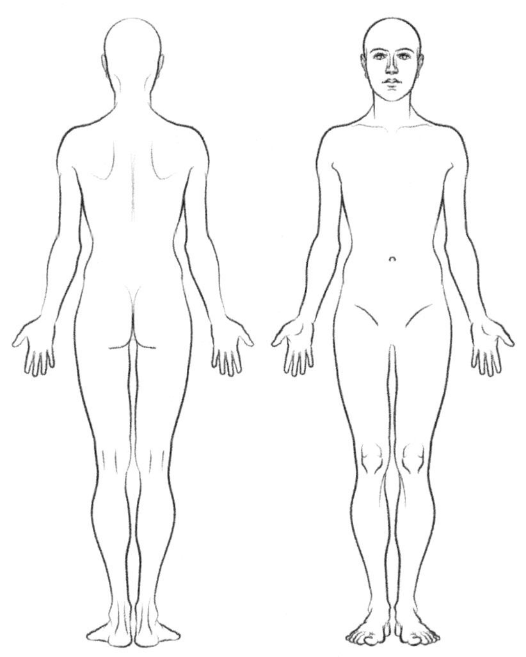

Pain Score
1 = Slight, 2 = Moderate, 3 = Severe.

	Left	Right
Jaw		
Neck		
Shoulder Girdle		
Chest		
Upper Back		
Lower Back		
Upper Arm		
Lower Arm		
Abdomen		
Hip / Buttock		
Upper Leg		
Lower Leg		

Notes

Today I Experienced			
Headache / Migraine		Diarrhoea	
Muscle Twinges / Cramps		Constipation	
Muscle Weakness		Bloating / Stomach Pain / IBS	
Skin Itching / Burning / Hives / Rash (circle all that apply)		Bladder Issues	
Bruising		Swelling	
Sweating		Stress	
Nervousness		Nausea / vomiting	
Sensitive to Sensory Stimulation (light / noise / temperature)		Numbness / Tingling (name part of body)	
Dizziness		Missed meal / unusual food	
Loss of appetite		Hormonal Changes	
Other:		Other:	
Other:		Other:	

Date: ***Weather:***

Hours Slept: Insomnia? Yes ☐ No ☐

How did you feel on waking today? I felt refreshed: ☐

Slightly unrefreshed: ☐ Moderately unrefreshed: ☐ Severely unrefreshed: ☐

Did you exercise today? Yes ☐ No ☐

		Morning	Afternoon	Evening
Fatigue	3			
	2			
	1			
	0			
Pain Levels	3			
	2			
	1			
	0			
Cognitive Symptoms / Brain Fog	3			
	2			
	1			
	0			

		Morning	Afternoon	Evening
Anxiety / Low Mood	3			
	2			
	1			
	0			
Activity Levels	3			
	2			
	1			
	0			
Other	3			
	2			
	1			
	0			

Symptom Score: 0 = No problem, 1 = Slight, 2 = Moderate, 3 = Severe. See p.3

Today's Notes:

Pain Location & Levels

Shade bodies, tick boxes or use pain score.

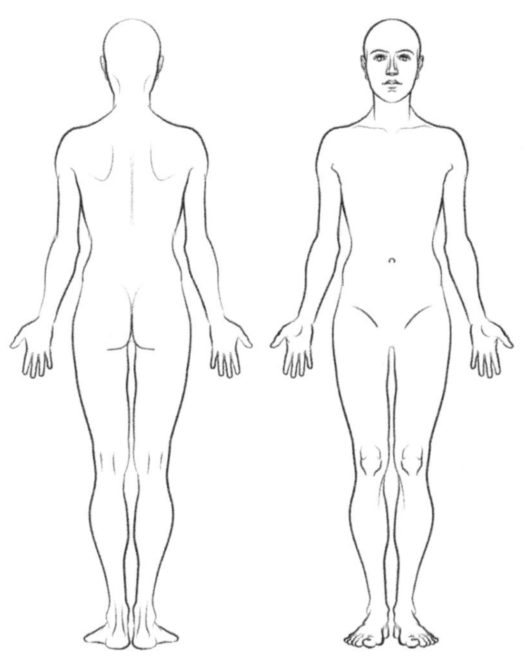

Pain Score
1 = Slight, 2 = Moderate, 3 = Severe.

	Left	Right
Jaw		
Neck		
Shoulder Girdle		
Chest		
Upper Back		
Lower Back		
Upper Arm		
Lower Arm		
Abdomen		
Hip / Buttock		
Upper Leg		
Lower Leg		

Notes

Today I Experienced			
Headache / Migraine		Diarrhoea	
Muscle Twinges / Cramps		Constipation	
Muscle Weakness		Bloating / Stomach Pain / IBS	
Skin Itching / Burning / Hives / Rash (circle all that apply)		Bladder Issues	
Bruising		Swelling	
Sweating		Stress	
Nervousness		Nausea / vomiting	
Sensitive to Sensory Stimulation (light / noise / temperature)		Numbness / Tingling (name part of body)	
Dizziness		Missed meal / unusual food	
Loss of appetite		Hormonal Changes	
Other:		Other:	
Other:		Other:	

Date: ***Weather:***

Hours Slept: Insomnia? Yes ☐ No ☐

How did you feel on waking today? I felt refreshed: ☐

Slightly unrefreshed: ☐ Moderately unrefreshed: ☐ Severely unrefreshed: ☐

Did you exercise today? Yes ☐ No ☐

		Morning	Afternoon	Evening
Fatigue	3			
	2			
	1			
	0			
Pain Levels	3			
	2			
	1			
	0			
Cognitive Symptoms / Brain Fog	3			
	2			
	1			
	0			

		Morning	Afternoon	Evening
Anxiety / Low Mood	3			
	2			
	1			
	0			
Activity Levels	3			
	2			
	1			
	0			
Other	3			
	2			
	1			
	0			

Symptom Score: 0 = No problem, 1 = Slight, 2 = Moderate, 3 = Severe. See p.3

Today's Notes:

Pain Location & Levels

Shade bodies, tick boxes or use pain score.

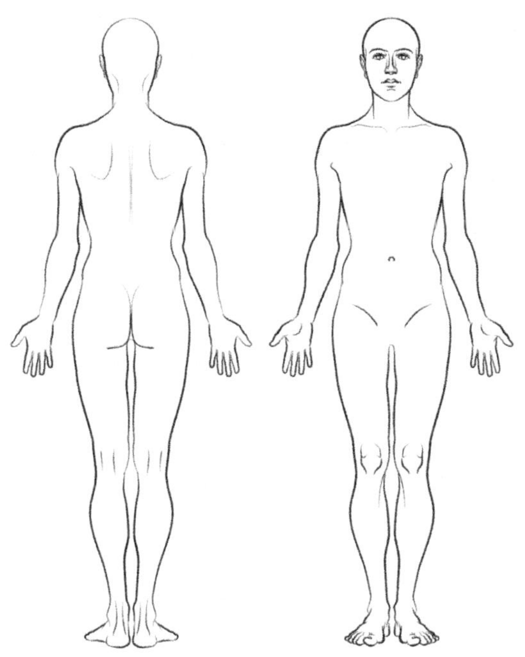

Pain Score
1 = Slight, 2 = Moderate, 3 = Severe.

	Left	Right
Jaw		
Neck		
Shoulder Girdle		
Chest		
Upper Back		
Lower Back		
Upper Arm		
Lower Arm		
Abdomen		
Hip / Buttock		
Upper Leg		
Lower Leg		

Notes

Today I Experienced			
Headache / Migraine		Diarrhoea	
Muscle Twinges / Cramps		Constipation	
Muscle Weakness		Bloating / Stomach Pain / IBS	
Skin Itching / Burning / Hives / Rash (circle all that apply)		Bladder Issues	
Bruising		Swelling	
Sweating		Stress	
Nervousness		Nausea / vomiting	
Sensitive to Sensory Stimulation (light / noise / temperature)		Numbness / Tingling (name part of body)	
Dizziness		Missed meal / unusual food	
Loss of appetite		Hormonal Changes	
Other:		Other:	
Other:		Other:	

Date: ***Weather:***

Hours Slept: Insomnia? Yes ☐ No ☐

How did you feel on waking today? I felt refreshed: ☐

Slightly unrefreshed: ☐ Moderately unrefreshed: ☐ Severely unrefreshed: ☐

Did you exercise today? Yes ☐ No ☐

		Morning	Afternoon	Evening
Fatigue	3			
	2			
	1			
	0			
Pain Levels	3			
	2			
	1			
	0			
Cognitive Symptoms / Brain Fog	3			
	2			
	1			
	0			

		Morning	Afternoon	Evening
Anxiety / Low Mood	3			
	2			
	1			
	0			
Activity Levels	3			
	2			
	1			
	0			
Other	3			
	2			
	1			
	0			

Symptom Score: 0 = No problem, 1 = Slight, 2 = Moderate, 3 = Severe. See p.3

Today's Notes:

Pain Location & Levels

Shade bodies, tick boxes or use pain score.

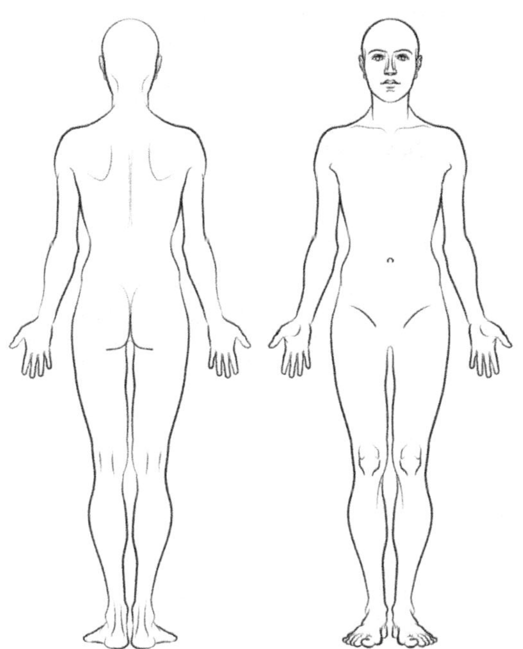

Pain Score
1 = Slight, 2 = Moderate, 3 = Severe.

	Left	Right
Jaw		
Neck		
Shoulder Girdle		
Chest		
Upper Back		
Lower Back		
Upper Arm		
Lower Arm		
Abdomen		
Hip / Buttock		
Upper Leg		
Lower Leg		

Notes

Today I Experienced			
Headache / Migraine		Diarrhoea	
Muscle Twinges / Cramps		Constipation	
Muscle Weakness		Bloating / Stomach Pain / IBS	
Skin Itching / Burning / Hives / Rash (circle all that apply)		Bladder Issues	
Bruising		Swelling	
Sweating		Stress	
Nervousness		Nausea / vomiting	
Sensitive to Sensory Stimulation (light / noise / temperature)		Numbness / Tingling (name part of body)	
Dizziness		Missed meal / unusual food	
Loss of appetite		Hormonal Changes	
Other:		Other:	
Other:		Other:	

Date: ***Weather:***

Hours Slept: Insomnia? Yes ☐ No ☐

How did you feel on waking today? I felt refreshed: ☐

Slightly unrefreshed: ☐ Moderately unrefreshed: ☐ Severely unrefreshed: ☐

Did you exercise today? Yes ☐ No ☐

		Morning	Afternoon	Evening
	3			
	2			
	1			
Fatigue	0			
	3			
	2			
	1			
Pain Levels	0			
	3			
	2			
	1			
Cognitive Symptoms / Brain Fog	0			

		Morning	Afternoon	Evening
	3			
	2			
	1			
Anxiety / Low Mood	0			
	3			
	2			
	1			
Activity Levels	0			
	3			
	2			
	1			
Other	0			

Symptom Score: 0 = No problem, 1 = Slight, 2 = Moderate, 3 = Severe. See p.3

Today's Notes:

Pain Location & Levels

Shade bodies, tick boxes or use pain score.

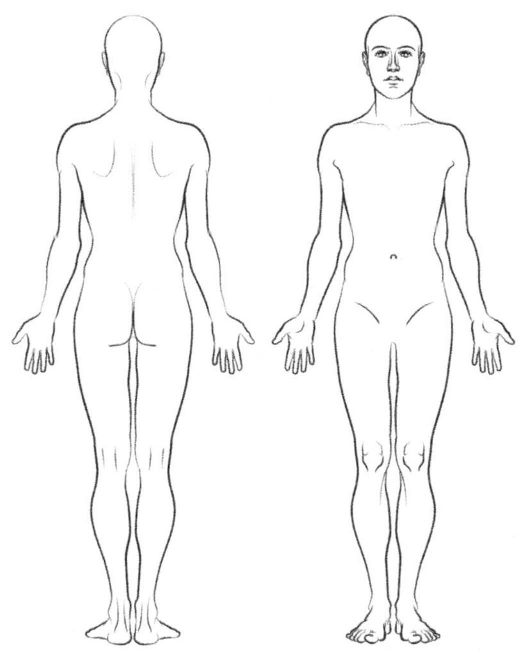

Pain Score
1 = Slight, 2 = Moderate, 3 = Severe.

	Left	Right
Jaw		
Neck		
Shoulder Girdle		
Chest		
Upper Back		
Lower Back		
Upper Arm		
Lower Arm		
Abdomen		
Hip / Buttock		
Upper Leg		
Lower Leg		

Notes

Today I Experienced			
Headache / Migraine		Diarrhoea	
Muscle Twinges / Cramps		Constipation	
Muscle Weakness		Bloating / Stomach Pain / IBS	
Skin Itching / Burning / Hives / Rash (circle all that apply)		Bladder Issues	
Bruising		Swelling	
Sweating		Stress	
Nervousness		Nausea / vomiting	
Sensitive to Sensory Stimulation (light / noise / temperature)		Numbness / Tingling (name part of body)	
Dizziness		Missed meal / unusual food	
Loss of appetite		Hormonal Changes	
Other:		Other:	
Other:		Other:	

Date: ___________ ***Weather:*** ___________

Hours Slept: ___________ Insomnia? Yes ☐ No ☐

How did you feel on waking today? I felt refreshed: ☐

Slightly unrefreshed: ☐ Moderately unrefreshed: ☐ Severely unrefreshed: ☐

Did you exercise today? Yes ☐ No ☐ ___________

		Morning	Afternoon	Evening
Fatigue	3			
	2			
	1			
	0			
Pain Levels	3			
	2			
	1			
	0			
Cognitive Symptoms / Brain Fog	3			
	2			
	1			
	0			

		Morning	Afternoon	Evening
Anxiety / Low Mood	3			
	2			
	1			
	0			
Activity Levels	3			
	2			
	1			
	0			
Other	3			
	2			
	1			
	0			

Symptom Score: 0 = No problem, 1 = Slight, 2 = Moderate, 3 = Severe. See p.3

Today's Notes:

Pain Location & Levels

Shade bodies, tick boxes or use pain score.

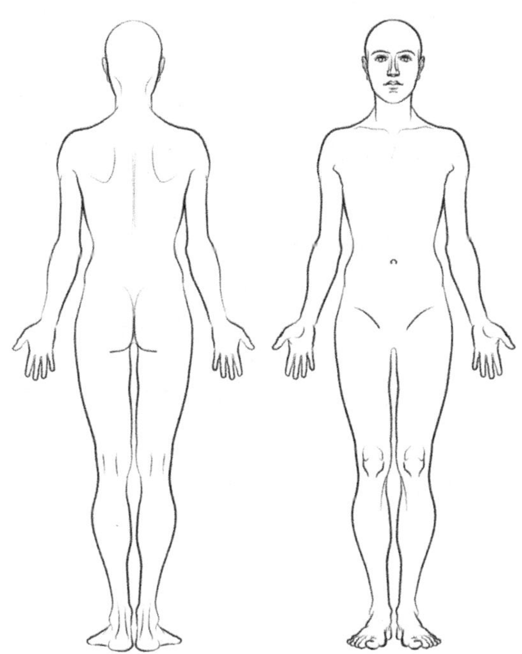

Pain Score
1 = Slight, 2 = Moderate, 3 = Severe.

	Left	Right
Jaw		
Neck		
Shoulder Girdle		
Chest		
Upper Back		
Lower Back		
Upper Arm		
Lower Arm		
Abdomen		
Hip / Buttock		
Upper Leg		
Lower Leg		

Notes

Today I Experienced			
Headache / Migraine		Diarrhoea	
Muscle Twinges / Cramps		Constipation	
Muscle Weakness		Bloating / Stomach Pain / IBS	
Skin Itching / Burning / Hives / Rash (circle all that apply)		Bladder Issues	
Bruising		Swelling	
Sweating		Stress	
Nervousness		Nausea / vomiting	
Sensitive to Sensory Stimulation (light / noise / temperature)		Numbness / Tingling (name part of body)	
Dizziness		Missed meal / unusual food	
Loss of appetite		Hormonal Changes	
Other:		Other:	
Other:		Other:	

Date: ***Weather:***

Hours Slept: Insomnia? Yes ☐ No ☐

How did you feel on waking today? I felt refreshed: ☐

Slightly unrefreshed: ☐ Moderately unrefreshed: ☐ Severely unrefreshed: ☐

Did you exercise today? Yes ☐ No ☐

		Morning	Afternoon	Evening
Fatigue	3			
	2			
	1			
	0			
Pain Levels	3			
	2			
	1			
	0			
Cognitive Symptoms / Brain Fog	3			
	2			
	1			
	0			

		Morning	Afternoon	Evening
Anxiety / Low Mood	3			
	2			
	1			
	0			
Activity Levels	3			
	2			
	1			
	0			
Other	3			
	2			
	1			
	0			

Symptom Score: 0 = No problem, 1 = Slight, 2 = Moderate, 3 = Severe. See p.3

Today's Notes:

Pain Location & Levels

Shade bodies, tick boxes or use pain score.

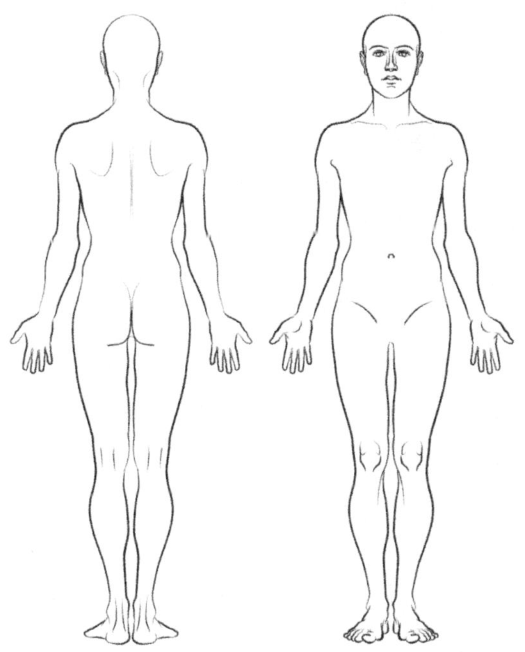

Pain Score
1 = Slight, 2 = Moderate, 3 = Severe.

	Left	Right
Jaw		
Neck		
Shoulder Girdle		
Chest		
Upper Back		
Lower Back		
Upper Arm		
Lower Arm		
Abdomen		
Hip / Buttock		
Upper Leg		
Lower Leg		

Notes

Today I Experienced			
Headache / Migraine		Diarrhoea	
Muscle Twinges / Cramps		Constipation	
Muscle Weakness		Bloating / Stomach Pain / IBS	
Skin Itching / Burning / Hives / Rash (circle all that apply)		Bladder Issues	
Bruising		Swelling	
Sweating		Stress	
Nervousness		Nausea / vomiting	
Sensitive to Sensory Stimulation (light / noise / temperature)		Numbness / Tingling (name part of body)	
Dizziness		Missed meal / unusual food	
Loss of appetite		Hormonal Changes	
Other:		Other:	
Other:		Other:	

Date: ______ ***Weather:*** ______

Hours Slept: ______ Insomnia? Yes ☐ No ☐

How did you feel on waking today? I felt refreshed: ☐

Slightly unrefreshed: ☐ Moderately unrefreshed: ☐ Severely unrefreshed: ☐

Did you exercise today? Yes ☐ No ☐ ______

		Morning	Afternoon	Evening
	3			
	2			
	1			
Fatigue	0			
	3			
	2			
	1			
Pain Levels	0			
	3			
Cognitive Symptoms / Brain Fog	2			
	1			
	0			

		Morning	Afternoon	Evening
	3			
	2			
Anxiety / Low Mood	1			
	0			
	3			
	2			
	1			
Activity Levels	0			
	3			
	2			
	1			
Other	0			

Symptom Score: 0 = No problem, 1 = Slight, 2 = Moderate, 3 = Severe. See p.3

Today's Notes:

Pain Location & Levels

Shade bodies, tick boxes or use pain score.

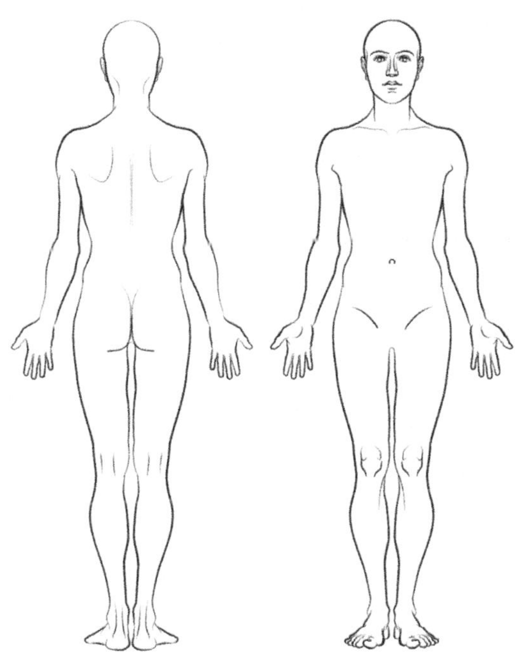

Pain Score
1 = Slight, 2 = Moderate, 3 = Severe.

	Left	Right
Jaw		
Neck		
Shoulder Girdle		
Chest		
Upper Back		
Lower Back		
Upper Arm		
Lower Arm		
Abdomen		
Hip / Buttock		
Upper Leg		
Lower Leg		

Notes

Today I Experienced			
Headache / Migraine		Diarrhoea	
Muscle Twinges / Cramps		Constipation	
Muscle Weakness		Bloating / Stomach Pain / IBS	
Skin Itching / Burning / Hives / Rash (circle all that apply)		Bladder Issues	
Bruising		Swelling	
Sweating		Stress	
Nervousness		Nausea / vomiting	
Sensitive to Sensory Stimulation (light / noise / temperature)		Numbness / Tingling (name part of body)	
Dizziness		Missed meal / unusual food	
Loss of appetite		Hormonal Changes	
Other:		Other:	
Other:		Other:	

Date: ***Weather:***

Hours Slept: Insomnia? Yes ☐ No ☐

How did you feel on waking today? I felt refreshed: ☐

Slightly unrefreshed: ☐ Moderately unrefreshed: ☐ Severely unrefreshed: ☐

Did you exercise today? Yes ☐ No ☐

		Morning	Afternoon	Evening
	3			
	2			
	1			
Fatigue	0			
	3			
	2			
	1			
Pain Levels	0			
	3			
	2			
	1			
Cognitive Symptoms / Brain Fog	0			

		Morning	Afternoon	Evening
	3			
	2			
	1			
Anxiety / Low Mood	0			
	3			
	2			
	1			
Activity Levels	0			
	3			
	2			
	1			
Other	0			

Symptom Score: 0 = No problem, 1 = Slight, 2 = Moderate, 3 = Severe. See p.3

Today's Notes:

Pain Location & Levels

Shade bodies, tick boxes or use pain score.

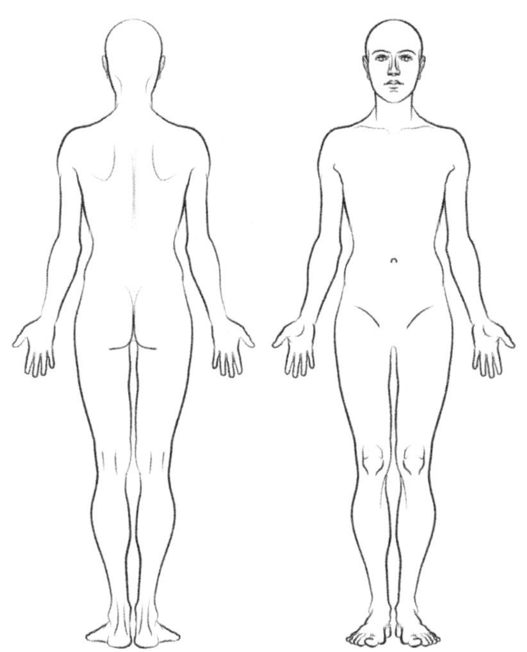

Pain Score
1 = Slight, 2 = Moderate, 3 = Severe.

	Left	Right
Jaw		
Neck		
Shoulder Girdle		
Chest		
Upper Back		
Lower Back		
Upper Arm		
Lower Arm		
Abdomen		
Hip / Buttock		
Upper Leg		
Lower Leg		

Notes

Today I Experienced			
Headache / Migraine		Diarrhoea	
Muscle Twinges / Cramps		Constipation	
Muscle Weakness		Bloating / Stomach Pain / IBS	
Skin Itching / Burning / Hives / Rash (circle all that apply)		Bladder Issues	
Bruising		Swelling	
Sweating		Stress	
Nervousness		Nausea / vomiting	
Sensitive to Sensory Stimulation (light / noise / temperature)		Numbness / Tingling (name part of body)	
Dizziness		Missed meal / unusual food	
Loss of appetite		Hormonal Changes	
Other:		Other:	
Other:		Other:	

Date: ***Weather:***

Hours Slept: Insomnia? Yes ☐ No ☐

How did you feel on waking today? I felt refreshed: ☐

Slightly unrefreshed: ☐ Moderately unrefreshed: ☐ Severely unrefreshed: ☐

Did you exercise today? Yes ☐ No ☐

		Morning	Afternoon	Evening
Fatigue	3			
	2			
	1			
	0			
Pain Levels	3			
	2			
	1			
	0			
Cognitive Symptoms / Brain Fog	3			
	2			
	1			
	0			

		Morning	Afternoon	Evening
Anxiety / Low Mood	3			
	2			
	1			
	0			
Activity Levels	3			
	2			
	1			
	0			
Other	3			
	2			
	1			
	0			

Symptom Score: 0 = No problem, 1 = Slight, 2 = Moderate, 3 = Severe. See p.3

Today's Notes:

Pain Location & Levels

Shade bodies, tick boxes or use pain score.

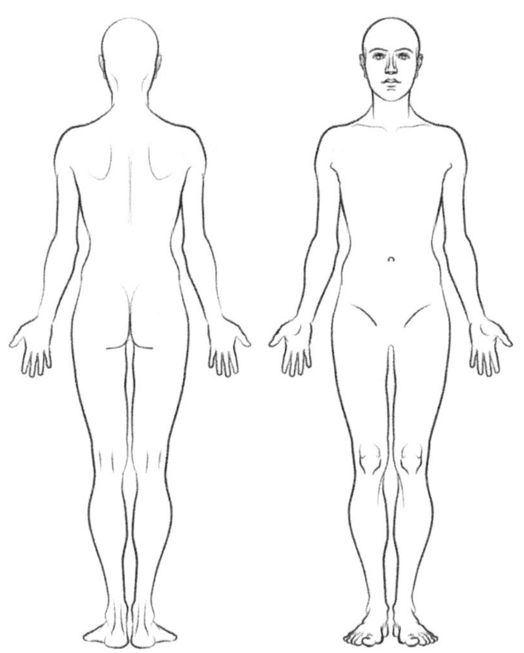

Pain Score
1 = Slight, 2 = Moderate, 3 = Severe.

	Left	Right
Jaw		
Neck		
Shoulder Girdle		
Chest		
Upper Back		
Lower Back		
Upper Arm		
Lower Arm		
Abdomen		
Hip / Buttock		
Upper Leg		
Lower Leg		

Notes

Today I Experienced			
Headache / Migraine		Diarrhoea	
Muscle Twinges / Cramps		Constipation	
Muscle Weakness		Bloating / Stomach Pain / IBS	
Skin Itching / Burning / Hives / Rash (circle all that apply)		Bladder Issues	
Bruising		Swelling	
Sweating		Stress	
Nervousness		Nausea / vomiting	
Sensitive to Sensory Stimulation (light / noise / temperature)		Numbness / Tingling (name part of body)	
Dizziness		Missed meal / unusual food	
Loss of appetite		Hormonal Changes	
Other:		Other:	
Other:		Other:	

Date: ***Weather:***

Hours Slept: Insomnia? Yes ☐ No ☐

How did you feel on waking today? I felt refreshed: ☐

Slightly unrefreshed: ☐ Moderately unrefreshed: ☐ Severely unrefreshed: ☐

Did you exercise today? Yes ☐ No ☐

		Morning	Afternoon	Evening
Fatigue	3			
	2			
	1			
	0			
Pain Levels	3			
	2			
	1			
	0			
Cognitive Symptoms / Brain Fog	3			
	2			
	1			
	0			

		Morning	Afternoon	Evening
Anxiety / Low Mood	3			
	2			
	1			
	0			
Activity Levels	3			
	2			
	1			
	0			
Other	3			
	2			
	1			
	0			

Symptom Score: 0 = No problem, 1 = Slight, 2 = Moderate, 3 = Severe. See p.3

Today's Notes:

Pain Location & Levels

Shade bodies, tick boxes or use pain score.

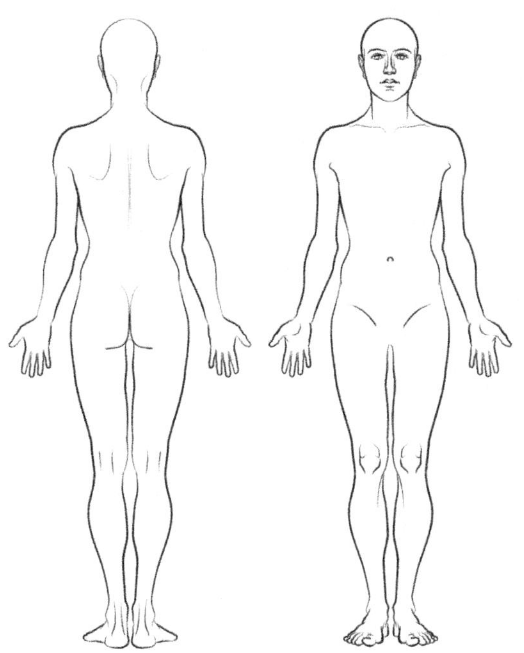

Pain Score
1 = Slight, 2 = Moderate, 3 = Severe.

	Left	Right
Jaw		
Neck		
Shoulder Girdle		
Chest		
Upper Back		
Lower Back		
Upper Arm		
Lower Arm		
Abdomen		
Hip / Buttock		
Upper Leg		
Lower Leg		

Notes

Today I Experienced			
Headache / Migraine		Diarrhoea	
Muscle Twinges / Cramps		Constipation	
Muscle Weakness		Bloating / Stomach Pain / IBS	
Skin Itching / Burning / Hives / Rash (circle all that apply)		Bladder Issues	
Bruising		Swelling	
Sweating		Stress	
Nervousness		Nausea / vomiting	
Sensitive to Sensory Stimulation (light / noise / temperature)		Numbness / Tingling (name part of body)	
Dizziness		Missed meal / unusual food	
Loss of appetite		Hormonal Changes	
Other:		Other:	
Other:		Other:	

Date: ***Weather:***

Hours Slept: Insomnia? Yes ☐ No ☐

How did you feel on waking today? I felt refreshed: ☐

Slightly unrefreshed: ☐ Moderately unrefreshed: ☐ Severely unrefreshed: ☐

Did you exercise today? Yes ☐ No ☐

		Morning	Afternoon	Evening
Fatigue	3			
	2			
	1			
	0			
Pain Levels	3			
	2			
	1			
	0			
Cognitive Symptoms / Brain Fog	3			
	2			
	1			
	0			

		Morning	Afternoon	Evening
Anxiety / Low Mood	3			
	2			
	1			
	0			
Activity Levels	3			
	2			
	1			
	0			
Other	3			
	2			
	1			
	0			

Symptom Score: 0 = No problem, 1 = Slight, 2 = Moderate, 3 = Severe. See p.3

Today's Notes:

Pain Location & Levels

Shade bodies, tick boxes or use pain score.

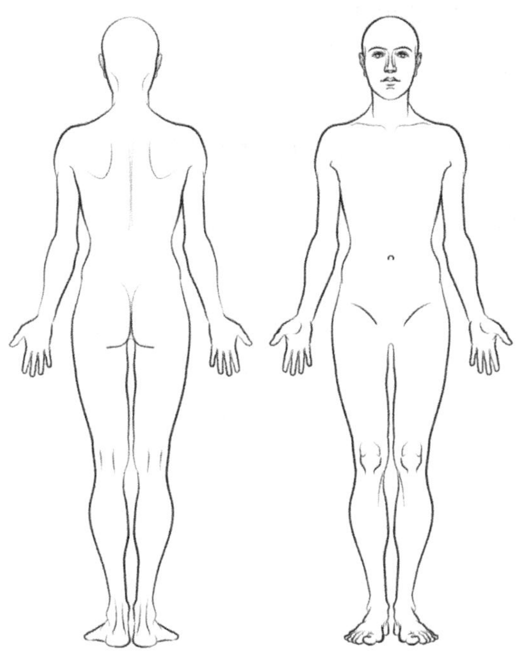

Pain Score
1 = Slight, 2 = Moderate, 3 = Severe.

	Left	Right
Jaw		
Neck		
Shoulder Girdle		
Chest		
Upper Back		
Lower Back		
Upper Arm		
Lower Arm		
Abdomen		
Hip / Buttock		
Upper Leg		
Lower Leg		

Notes

Today I Experienced			
Headache / Migraine		Diarrhoea	
Muscle Twinges / Cramps		Constipation	
Muscle Weakness		Bloating / Stomach Pain / IBS	
Skin Itching / Burning / Hives / Rash (circle all that apply)		Bladder Issues	
Bruising		Swelling	
Sweating		Stress	
Nervousness		Nausea / vomiting	
Sensitive to Sensory Stimulation (light / noise / temperature)		Numbness / Tingling (name part of body)	
Dizziness		Missed meal / unusual food	
Loss of appetite		Hormonal Changes	
Other:		Other:	
Other:		Other:	

Date: ***Weather:***

Hours Slept: Insomnia? Yes ☐ No ☐

How did you feel on waking today? I felt refreshed: ☐

Slightly unrefreshed: ☐ Moderately unrefreshed: ☐ Severely unrefreshed: ☐

Did you exercise today? Yes ☐ No ☐

		Morning	Afternoon	Evening
Fatigue	3			
	2			
	1			
	0			
Pain Levels	3			
	2			
	1			
	0			
Cognitive Symptoms / Brain Fog	3			
	2			
	1			
	0			

		Morning	Afternoon	Evening
Anxiety / Low Mood	3			
	2			
	1			
	0			
Activity Levels	3			
	2			
	1			
	0			
Other	3			
	2			
	1			
	0			

Symptom Score: 0 = No problem, 1 = Slight, 2 = Moderate, 3 = Severe. See p.3

Today's Notes:

Pain Location & Levels

Shade bodies, tick boxes or use pain score.

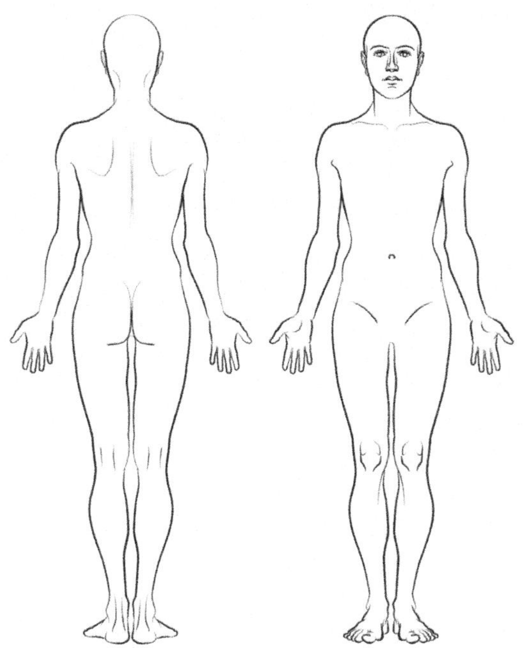

Pain Score
1 = Slight, 2 = Moderate, 3 = Severe.

	Left	Right
Jaw		
Neck		
Shoulder Girdle		
Chest		
Upper Back		
Lower Back		
Upper Arm		
Lower Arm		
Abdomen		
Hip / Buttock		
Upper Leg		
Lower Leg		

Notes

Today I Experienced			
Headache / Migraine		Diarrhoea	
Muscle Twinges / Cramps		Constipation	
Muscle Weakness		Bloating / Stomach Pain / IBS	
Skin Itching / Burning / Hives / Rash (circle all that apply)		Bladder Issues	
Bruising		Swelling	
Sweating		Stress	
Nervousness		Nausea / vomiting	
Sensitive to Sensory Stimulation (light / noise / temperature)		Numbness / Tingling (name part of body)	
Dizziness		Missed meal / unusual food	
Loss of appetite		Hormonal Changes	
Other:		Other:	
Other:		Other:	

Date: ***Weather:***

Hours Slept: Insomnia? Yes ☐ No ☐

How did you feel on waking today? I felt refreshed: ☐

Slightly unrefreshed: ☐ Moderately unrefreshed: ☐ Severely unrefreshed: ☐

Did you exercise today? Yes ☐ No ☐

		Morning	Afternoon	Evening
	3			
	2			
	1			
Fatigue	0			
	3			
	2			
	1			
Pain Levels	0			
	3			
	2			
	1			
Cognitive Symptoms / Brain Fog	0			

		Morning	Afternoon	Evening
	3			
	2			
	1			
Anxiety / Low Mood	0			
	3			
	2			
	1			
Activity Levels	0			
	3			
	2			
	1			
Other	0			

Symptom Score: 0 = No problem, 1 = Slight, 2 = Moderate, 3 = Severe. See p.3

Today's Notes:

Pain Location & Levels

Shade bodies, tick boxes or use pain score.

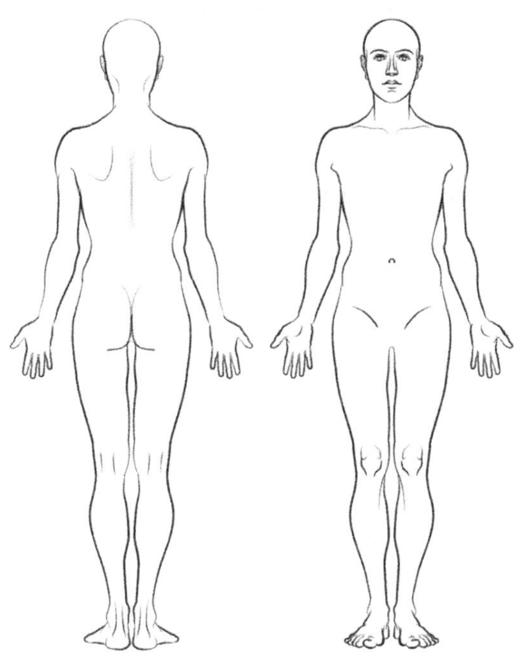

Pain Score
1 = Slight, 2 = Moderate, 3 = Severe.

	Left	Right
Jaw		
Neck		
Shoulder Girdle		
Chest		
Upper Back		
Lower Back		
Upper Arm		
Lower Arm		
Abdomen		
Hip / Buttock		
Upper Leg		
Lower Leg		

Notes

Today I Experienced			
Headache / Migraine		Diarrhoea	
Muscle Twinges / Cramps		Constipation	
Muscle Weakness		Bloating / Stomach Pain / IBS	
Skin Itching / Burning / Hives / Rash (circle all that apply)		Bladder Issues	
Bruising		Swelling	
Sweating		Stress	
Nervousness		Nausea / vomiting	
Sensitive to Sensory Stimulation (light / noise / temperature)		Numbness / Tingling (name part of body)	
Dizziness		Missed meal / unusual food	
Loss of appetite		Hormonal Changes	
Other:		Other:	
Other:		Other:	

Date: ______________ ***Weather:*** ______________

Hours Slept: ______________ Insomnia? Yes ☐ No ☐

How did you feel on waking today? I felt refreshed: ☐

Slightly unrefreshed: ☐ Moderately unrefreshed: ☐ Severely unrefreshed: ☐

Did you exercise today? Yes ☐ No ☐ ______________

		Morning	Afternoon	Evening
	3			
	2			
	1			
Fatigue	0			
	3			
	2			
Pain	1			
Levels	0			
	3			
Cognitive	2			
Symptoms	1			
/ Brain Fog	0			

		Morning	Afternoon	Evening
	3			
Anxiety /	2			
Low	1			
Mood	0			
	3			
	2			
Activity	1			
Levels	0			
	3			
	2			
	1			
Other	0			

Symptom Score: 0 = No problem, 1 = Slight, 2 = Moderate, 3 = Severe. See p.3

Today's Notes:

Pain Location & Levels

Shade bodies, tick boxes or use pain score.

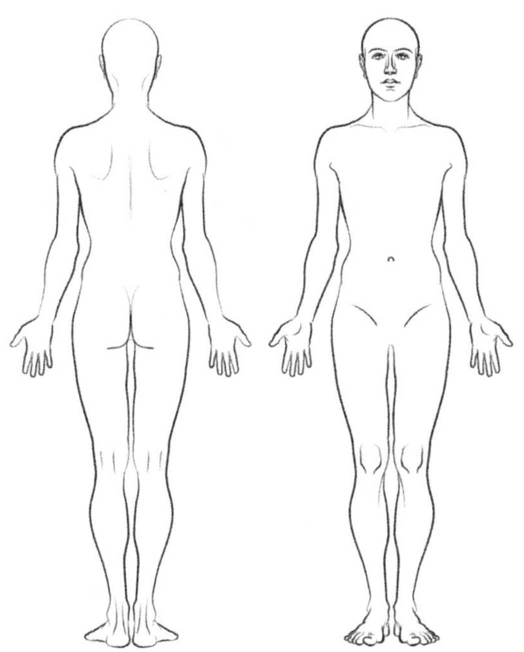

Pain Score
1 = Slight, 2 = Moderate, 3 = Severe.

	Left	Right
Jaw		
Neck		
Shoulder Girdle		
Chest		
Upper Back		
Lower Back		
Upper Arm		
Lower Arm		
Abdomen		
Hip / Buttock		
Upper Leg		
Lower Leg		

Notes

Today I Experienced			
Headache / Migraine		Diarrhoea	
Muscle Twinges / Cramps		Constipation	
Muscle Weakness		Bloating / Stomach Pain / IBS	
Skin Itching / Burning / Hives / Rash (circle all that apply)		Bladder Issues	
Bruising		Swelling	
Sweating		Stress	
Nervousness		Nausea / vomiting	
Sensitive to Sensory Stimulation (light / noise / temperature)		Numbness / Tingling (name part of body)	
Dizziness		Missed meal / unusual food	
Loss of appetite		Hormonal Changes	
Other:		Other:	
Other:		Other:	

Date: ___________ ***Weather:*** ___________

Hours Slept: ___________ Insomnia? Yes ☐ No ☐

How did you feel on waking today? I felt refreshed: ☐

Slightly unrefreshed: ☐ Moderately unrefreshed: ☐ Severely unrefreshed: ☐

Did you exercise today? Yes ☐ No ☐ ___________

		Morning	Afternoon	Evening
Fatigue	3			
	2			
	1			
	0			
Pain Levels	3			
	2			
	1			
	0			
Cognitive Symptoms / Brain Fog	3			
	2			
	1			
	0			

		Morning	Afternoon	Evening
Anxiety / Low Mood	3			
	2			
	1			
	0			
Activity Levels	3			
	2			
	1			
	0			
Other	3			
	2			
	1			
	0			

Symptom Score: 0 = No problem, 1 = Slight, 2 = Moderate, 3 = Severe. See p.3

Today's Notes:

Pain Location & Levels

Shade bodies, tick boxes or use pain score.

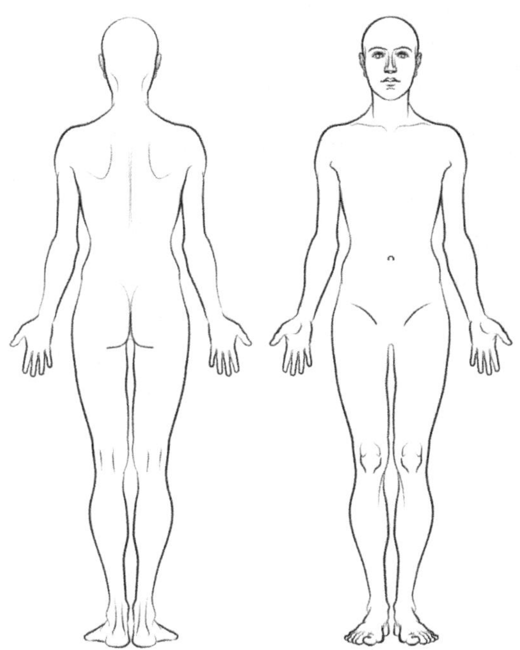

Pain Score
1 = Slight, 2 = Moderate, 3 = Severe.

	Left	Right
Jaw		
Neck		
Shoulder Girdle		
Chest		
Upper Back		
Lower Back		
Upper Arm		
Lower Arm		
Abdomen		
Hip / Buttock		
Upper Leg		
Lower Leg		

Notes

Today I Experienced			
Headache / Migraine		Diarrhoea	
Muscle Twinges / Cramps		Constipation	
Muscle Weakness		Bloating / Stomach Pain / IBS	
Skin Itching / Burning / Hives / Rash (circle all that apply)		Bladder Issues	
Bruising		Swelling	
Sweating		Stress	
Nervousness		Nausea / vomiting	
Sensitive to Sensory Stimulation (light / noise / temperature)		Numbness / Tingling (name part of body)	
Dizziness		Missed meal / unusual food	
Loss of appetite		Hormonal Changes	
Other:		Other:	
Other:		Other:	

Date: ***Weather:***

Hours Slept: Insomnia? Yes ☐ No ☐

How did you feel on waking today? I felt refreshed: ☐

Slightly unrefreshed: ☐ Moderately unrefreshed: ☐ Severely unrefreshed: ☐

Did you exercise today? Yes ☐ No ☐

		Morning	Afternoon	Evening
	3			
	2			
	1			
Fatigue	0			
	3			
	2			
	1			
Pain Levels	0			
	3			
	2			
	1			
Cognitive Symptoms / Brain Fog	0			

		Morning	Afternoon	Evening
	3			
	2			
	1			
Anxiety / Low Mood	0			
	3			
	2			
	1			
Activity Levels	0			
	3			
	2			
	1			
Other	0			

Symptom Score: 0 = No problem, 1 = Slight, 2 = Moderate, 3 = Severe. See p.3

Today's Notes:

Pain Location & Levels

Shade bodies, tick boxes or use pain score.

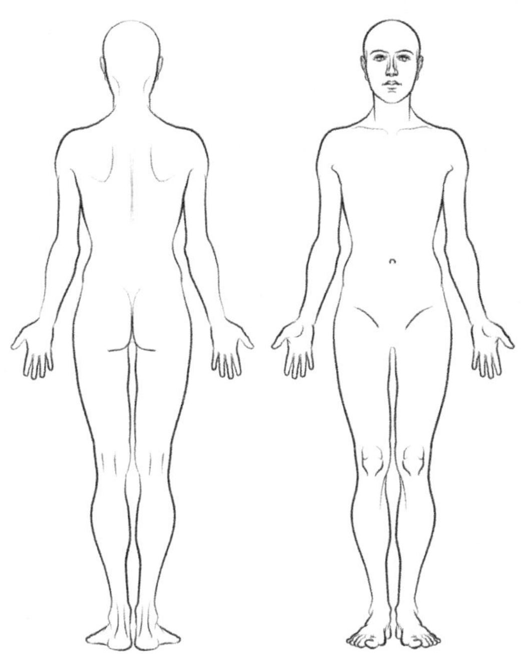

Pain Score
1 = Slight, 2 = Moderate, 3 = Severe.

	Left	Right
Jaw		
Neck		
Shoulder Girdle		
Chest		
Upper Back		
Lower Back		
Upper Arm		
Lower Arm		
Abdomen		
Hip / Buttock		
Upper Leg		
Lower Leg		

Notes

Today I Experienced			
Headache / Migraine		Diarrhoea	
Muscle Twinges / Cramps		Constipation	
Muscle Weakness		Bloating / Stomach Pain / IBS	
Skin Itching / Burning / Hives / Rash (circle all that apply)		Bladder Issues	
Bruising		Swelling	
Sweating		Stress	
Nervousness		Nausea / vomiting	
Sensitive to Sensory Stimulation (light / noise / temperature)		Numbness / Tingling (name part of body)	
Dizziness		Missed meal / unusual food	
Loss of appetite		Hormonal Changes	
Other:		Other:	
Other:		Other:	

Date: ***Weather:***

Hours Slept: Insomnia? Yes ☐ No ☐

How did you feel on waking today? I felt refreshed: ☐

Slightly unrefreshed: ☐ Moderately unrefreshed: ☐ Severely unrefreshed: ☐

Did you exercise today? Yes ☐ No ☐

		Morning	Afternoon	Evening
	3			
	2			
	1			
Fatigue	0			
	3			
	2			
Pain	1			
Levels	0			
	3			
Cognitive	2			
Symptoms / Brain	1			
Fog	0			

		Morning	Afternoon	Evening
	3			
Anxiety /	2			
Low	1			
Mood	0			
	3			
	2			
Activity	1			
Levels	0			
	3			
	2			
	1			
Other	0			

Symptom Score: 0 = No problem, 1 = Slight, 2 = Moderate, 3 = Severe. See p.3

Today's Notes:

Pain Location & Levels

Shade bodies, tick boxes or use pain score.

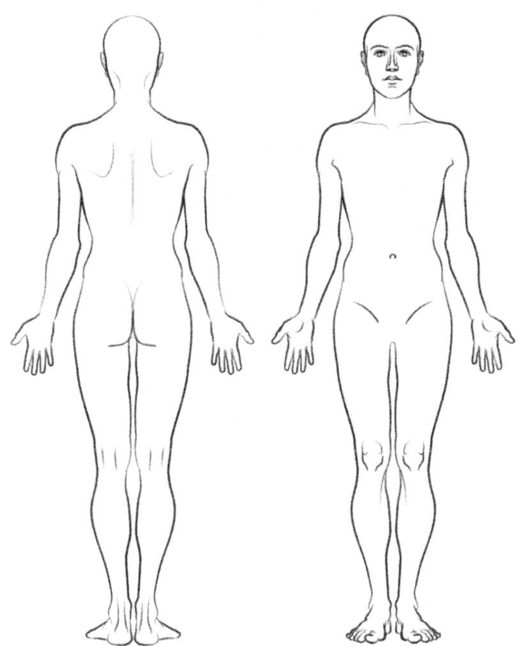

Pain Score
1 = Slight, 2 = Moderate, 3 = Severe.

	Left	Right
Jaw		
Neck		
Shoulder Girdle		
Chest		
Upper Back		
Lower Back		
Upper Arm		
Lower Arm		
Abdomen		
Hip / Buttock		
Upper Leg		
Lower Leg		

Notes

Today I Experienced			
Headache / Migraine		Diarrhoea	
Muscle Twinges / Cramps		Constipation	
Muscle Weakness		Bloating / Stomach Pain / IBS	
Skin Itching / Burning / Hives / Rash (circle all that apply)		Bladder Issues	
Bruising		Swelling	
Sweating		Stress	
Nervousness		Nausea / vomiting	
Sensitive to Sensory Stimulation (light / noise / temperature)		Numbness / Tingling (name part of body)	
Dizziness		Missed meal / unusual food	
Loss of appetite		Hormonal Changes	
Other:		Other:	
Other:		Other:	

Date: ***Weather:***

Hours Slept: Insomnia? Yes ☐ No ☐

How did you feel on waking today? I felt refreshed: ☐

Slightly unrefreshed: ☐ Moderately unrefreshed: ☐ Severely unrefreshed: ☐

Did you exercise today? Yes ☐ No ☐

		Morning	Afternoon	Evening
Fatigue	3			
	2			
	1			
	0			
Pain Levels	3			
	2			
	1			
	0			
Cognitive Symptoms / Brain Fog	3			
	2			
	1			
	0			

		Morning	Afternoon	Evening
Anxiety / Low Mood	3			
	2			
	1			
	0			
Activity Levels	3			
	2			
	1			
	0			
Other	3			
	2			
	1			
	0			

Symptom Score: 0 = No problem, 1 = Slight, 2 = Moderate, 3 = Severe. See p.3

Today's Notes:

Pain Location & Levels

Shade bodies, tick boxes or use pain score.

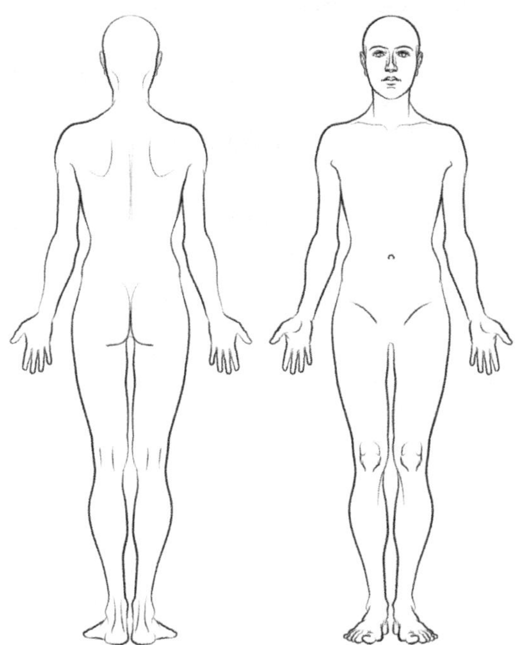

Pain Score
1 = Slight, 2 = Moderate, 3 = Severe.

	Left	Right
Jaw		
Neck		
Shoulder Girdle		
Chest		
Upper Back		
Lower Back		
Upper Arm		
Lower Arm		
Abdomen		
Hip / Buttock		
Upper Leg		
Lower Leg		

Notes

Today I Experienced			
Headache / Migraine		Diarrhoea	
Muscle Twinges / Cramps		Constipation	
Muscle Weakness		Bloating / Stomach Pain / IBS	
Skin Itching / Burning / Hives / Rash (circle all that apply)		Bladder Issues	
Bruising		Swelling	
Sweating		Stress	
Nervousness		Nausea / vomiting	
Sensitive to Sensory Stimulation (light / noise / temperature)		Numbness / Tingling (name part of body)	
Dizziness		Missed meal / unusual food	
Loss of appetite		Hormonal Changes	
Other:		Other:	
Other:		Other:	

Date: **Weather:**

Hours Slept: Insomnia? Yes ☐ No ☐

How did you feel on waking today? I felt refreshed: ☐

Slightly unrefreshed: ☐ Moderately unrefreshed: ☐ Severely unrefreshed: ☐

Did you exercise today? Yes ☐ No ☐

		Morning	Afternoon	Evening
Fatigue	3			
	2			
	1			
	0			
Pain Levels	3			
	2			
	1			
	0			
Cognitive Symptoms / Brain Fog	3			
	2			
	1			
	0			

		Morning	Afternoon	Evening
Anxiety / Low Mood	3			
	2			
	1			
	0			
Activity Levels	3			
	2			
	1			
	0			
Other	3			
	2			
	1			
	0			

Symptom Score: 0 = No problem, 1 = Slight, 2 = Moderate, 3 = Severe. See p.3

Today's Notes:

Pain Location & Levels

Shade bodies, tick boxes or use pain score.

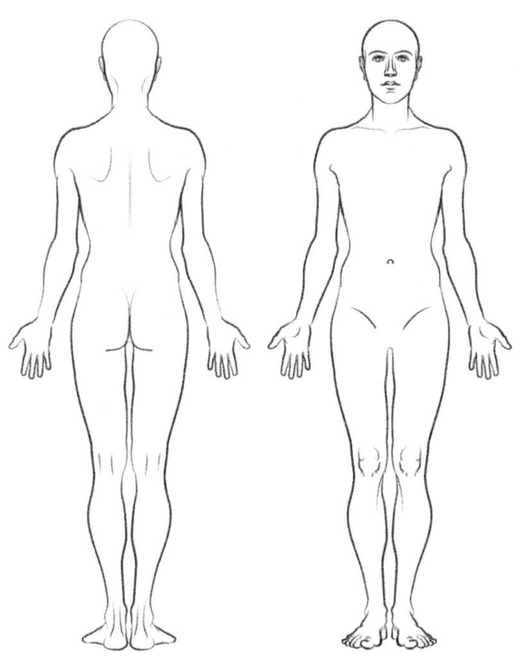

Pain Score
1 = Slight, 2 = Moderate, 3 = Severe.

	Left	Right
Jaw		
Neck		
Shoulder Girdle		
Chest		
Upper Back		
Lower Back		
Upper Arm		
Lower Arm		
Abdomen		
Hip / Buttock		
Upper Leg		
Lower Leg		

Notes

Today I Experienced			
Headache / Migraine		Diarrhoea	
Muscle Twinges / Cramps		Constipation	
Muscle Weakness		Bloating / Stomach Pain / IBS	
Skin Itching / Burning / Hives / Rash (circle all that apply)		Bladder Issues	
Bruising		Swelling	
Sweating		Stress	
Nervousness		Nausea / vomiting	
Sensitive to Sensory Stimulation (light / noise / temperature)		Numbness / Tingling (name part of body)	
Dizziness		Missed meal / unusual food	
Loss of appetite		Hormonal Changes	
Other:		Other:	
Other:		Other:	

Date: ***Weather:***

Hours Slept: Insomnia? Yes ☐ No ☐

How did you feel on waking today? I felt refreshed: ☐

Slightly unrefreshed: ☐ Moderately unrefreshed: ☐ Severely unrefreshed: ☐

Did you exercise today? Yes ☐ No ☐

		Morning	Afternoon	Evening			Morning	Afternoon	Evening
	3					3			
	2					2			
	1				*Anxiety / Low Mood*	1			
Fatigue	0					0			
	3					3			
	2					2			
	1					1			
Pain Levels	0				*Activity Levels*	0			
	3					3			
Cognitive Symptoms / Brain Fog	2					2			
	1					1			
	0				*Other*	0			

Symptom Score: 0 = No problem, 1 = Slight, 2 = Moderate, 3 = Severe. See p.3

Today's Notes:

Pain Location & Levels

Shade bodies, tick boxes or use pain score.

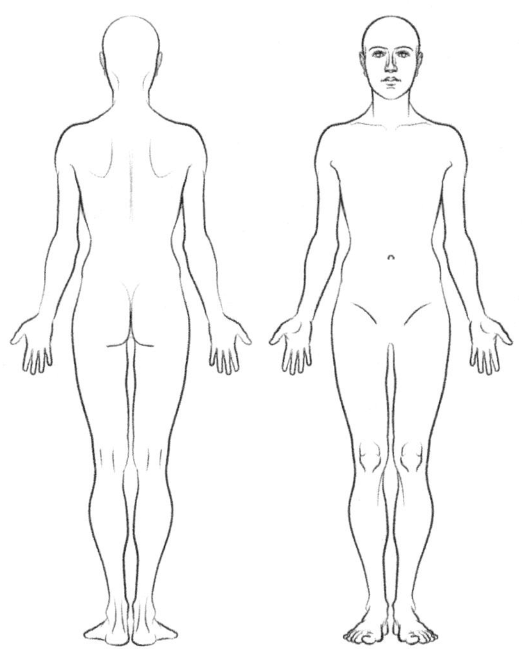

Pain Score
1 = Slight, 2 = Moderate, 3 = Severe.

	Left	Right
Jaw		
Neck		
Shoulder Girdle		
Chest		
Upper Back		
Lower Back		
Upper Arm		
Lower Arm		
Abdomen		
Hip / Buttock		
Upper Leg		
Lower Leg		

Notes

Today I Experienced			
Headache / Migraine		Diarrhoea	
Muscle Twinges / Cramps		Constipation	
Muscle Weakness		Bloating / Stomach Pain / IBS	
Skin Itching / Burning / Hives / Rash (circle all that apply)		Bladder Issues	
Bruising		Swelling	
Sweating		Stress	
Nervousness		Nausea / vomiting	
Sensitive to Sensory Stimulation (light / noise / temperature)		Numbness / Tingling (name part of body)	
Dizziness		Missed meal / unusual food	
Loss of appetite		Hormonal Changes	
Other:		Other:	
Other:		Other:	

Date: ***Weather:***

Hours Slept: Insomnia? Yes ☐ No ☐

How did you feel on waking today? I felt refreshed: ☐

Slightly unrefreshed: ☐ Moderately unrefreshed: ☐ Severely unrefreshed: ☐

Did you exercise today? Yes ☐ No ☐

		Morning	Afternoon	Evening
Fatigue	3			
	2			
	1			
	0			
Pain Levels	3			
	2			
	1			
	0			
Cognitive Symptoms / Brain Fog	3			
	2			
	1			
	0			

		Morning	Afternoon	Evening
Anxiety / Low Mood	3			
	2			
	1			
	0			
Activity Levels	3			
	2			
	1			
	0			
Other	3			
	2			
	1			
	0			

Symptom Score: 0 = No problem, 1 = Slight, 2 = Moderate, 3 = Severe. See p.3

Today's Notes:

Pain Location & Levels

Shade bodies, tick boxes or use pain score.

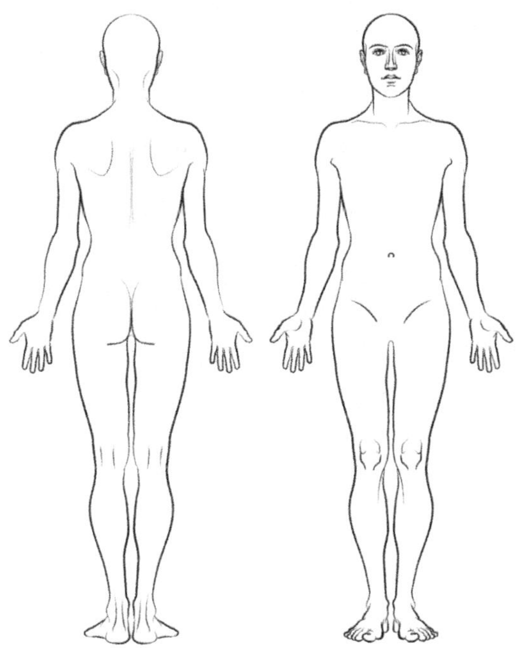

Pain Score
1 = Slight, 2 = Moderate, 3 = Severe.

	Left	Right
Jaw		
Neck		
Shoulder Girdle		
Chest		
Upper Back		
Lower Back		
Upper Arm		
Lower Arm		
Abdomen		
Hip / Buttock		
Upper Leg		
Lower Leg		

Notes

Today I Experienced			
Headache / Migraine		Diarrhoea	
Muscle Twinges / Cramps		Constipation	
Muscle Weakness		Bloating / Stomach Pain / IBS	
Skin Itching / Burning / Hives / Rash (circle all that apply)		Bladder Issues	
Bruising		Swelling	
Sweating		Stress	
Nervousness		Nausea / vomiting	
Sensitive to Sensory Stimulation (light / noise / temperature)		Numbness / Tingling (name part of body)	
Dizziness		Missed meal / unusual food	
Loss of appetite		Hormonal Changes	
Other:		Other:	
Other:		Other:	

Date: ***Weather:***

Hours Slept: Insomnia? Yes ☐ No ☐

How did you feel on waking today? I felt refreshed: ☐

Slightly unrefreshed: ☐ Moderately unrefreshed: ☐ Severely unrefreshed: ☐

Did you exercise today? Yes ☐ No ☐

		Morning	Afternoon	Evening
Fatigue	3			
	2			
	1			
	0			
Pain Levels	3			
	2			
	1			
	0			
Cognitive Symptoms / Brain Fog	3			
	2			
	1			
	0			

		Morning	Afternoon	Evening
Anxiety / Low Mood	3			
	2			
	1			
	0			
Activity Levels	3			
	2			
	1			
	0			
Other	3			
	2			
	1			
	0			

Symptom Score: 0 = No problem, 1 = Slight, 2 = Moderate, 3 = Severe. See p.3

Today's Notes:

Pain Location & Levels

Shade bodies, tick boxes or use pain score.

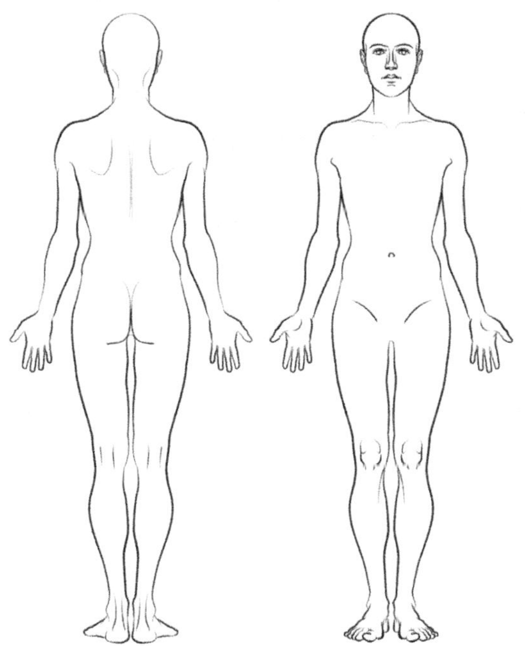

Pain Score
1 = Slight, 2 = Moderate, 3 = Severe.

	Left	Right
Jaw		
Neck		
Shoulder Girdle		
Chest		
Upper Back		
Lower Back		
Upper Arm		
Lower Arm		
Abdomen		
Hip / Buttock		
Upper Leg		
Lower Leg		

Notes

Today I Experienced			
Headache / Migraine		Diarrhoea	
Muscle Twinges / Cramps		Constipation	
Muscle Weakness		Bloating / Stomach Pain / IBS	
Skin Itching / Burning / Hives / Rash (circle all that apply)		Bladder Issues	
Bruising		Swelling	
Sweating		Stress	
Nervousness		Nausea / vomiting	
Sensitive to Sensory Stimulation (light / noise / temperature)		Numbness / Tingling (name part of body)	
Dizziness		Missed meal / unusual food	
Loss of appetite		Hormonal Changes	
Other:		Other:	
Other:		Other:	

Date: ***Weather:***

Hours Slept: Insomnia? Yes ☐ No ☐

How did you feel on waking today? I felt refreshed: ☐

Slightly unrefreshed: ☐ Moderately unrefreshed: ☐ Severely unrefreshed: ☐

Did you exercise today? Yes ☐ No ☐

		Morning	Afternoon	Evening
Fatigue	3			
	2			
	1			
	0			
Pain Levels	3			
	2			
	1			
	0			
Cognitive Symptoms / Brain Fog	3			
	2			
	1			
	0			

		Morning	Afternoon	Evening
Anxiety / Low Mood	3			
	2			
	1			
	0			
Activity Levels	3			
	2			
	1			
	0			
Other	3			
	2			
	1			
	0			

Symptom Score: 0 = No problem, 1 = Slight, 2 = Moderate, 3 = Severe. See p.3

Today's Notes:

Pain Location & Levels

Shade bodies, tick boxes or use pain score.

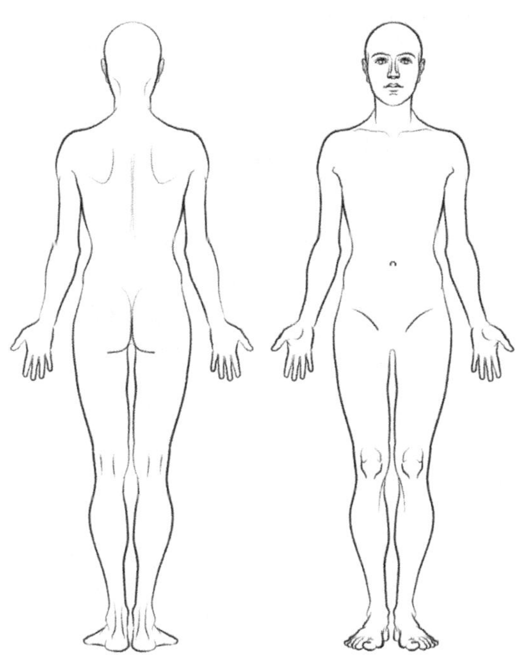

Pain Score
1 = Slight, 2 = Moderate, 3 = Severe.

	Left	Right
Jaw		
Neck		
Shoulder Girdle		
Chest		
Upper Back		
Lower Back		
Upper Arm		
Lower Arm		
Abdomen		
Hip / Buttock		
Upper Leg		
Lower Leg		

Notes

Today I Experienced			
Headache / Migraine		Diarrhoea	
Muscle Twinges / Cramps		Constipation	
Muscle Weakness		Bloating / Stomach Pain / IBS	
Skin Itching / Burning / Hives / Rash (circle all that apply)		Bladder Issues	
Bruising		Swelling	
Sweating		Stress	
Nervousness		Nausea / vomiting	
Sensitive to Sensory Stimulation (light / noise / temperature)		Numbness / Tingling (name part of body)	
Dizziness		Missed meal / unusual food	
Loss of appetite		Hormonal Changes	
Other:		Other:	
Other:		Other:	

Date: **Weather:**

Hours Slept: Insomnia? Yes ☐ No ☐

How did you feel on waking today? I felt refreshed: ☐

Slightly unrefreshed: ☐ Moderately unrefreshed: ☐ Severely unrefreshed: ☐

Did you exercise today? Yes ☐ No ☐

		Morning	Afternoon	Evening
Fatigue	3			
	2			
	1			
	0			
Pain Levels	3			
	2			
	1			
	0			
Cognitive Symptoms / Brain Fog	3			
	2			
	1			
	0			

		Morning	Afternoon	Evening
Anxiety / Low Mood	3			
	2			
	1			
	0			
Activity Levels	3			
	2			
	1			
	0			
Other	3			
	2			
	1			
	0			

Symptom Score: 0 = No problem, 1 = Slight, 2 = Moderate, 3 = Severe. See p.3

Today's Notes:

Pain Location & Levels

Shade bodies, tick boxes or use pain score.

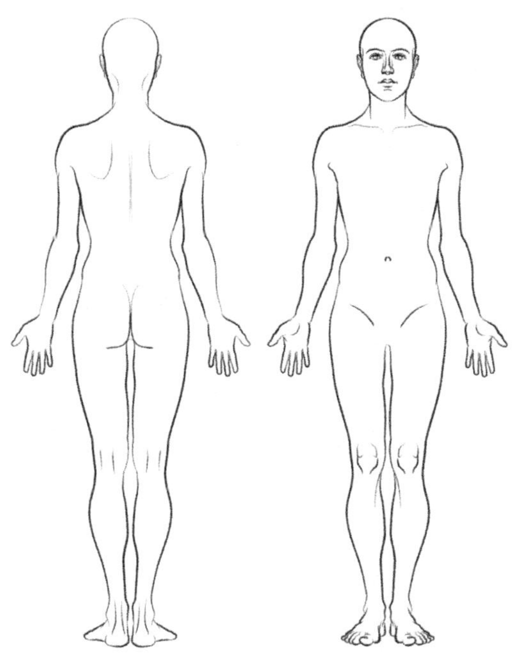

Pain Score
1 = Slight, 2 = Moderate, 3 = Severe.

	Left	Right
Jaw		
Neck		
Shoulder Girdle		
Chest		
Upper Back		
Lower Back		
Upper Arm		
Lower Arm		
Abdomen		
Hip / Buttock		
Upper Leg		
Lower Leg		

Notes

Today I Experienced			
Headache / Migraine		Diarrhoea	
Muscle Twinges / Cramps		Constipation	
Muscle Weakness		Bloating / Stomach Pain / IBS	
Skin Itching / Burning / Hives / Rash (circle all that apply)		Bladder Issues	
Bruising		Swelling	
Sweating		Stress	
Nervousness		Nausea / vomiting	
Sensitive to Sensory Stimulation (light / noise / temperature)		Numbness / Tingling (name part of body)	
Dizziness		Missed meal / unusual food	
Loss of appetite		Hormonal Changes	
Other:		Other:	
Other:		Other:	

Date: ***Weather:***

Hours Slept: Insomnia? Yes ☐ No ☐

How did you feel on waking today? I felt refreshed: ☐

Slightly unrefreshed: ☐ Moderately unrefreshed: ☐ Severely unrefreshed: ☐

Did you exercise today? Yes ☐ No ☐

		Morning	Afternoon	Evening
Fatigue	3			
	2			
	1			
	0			
Pain Levels	3			
	2			
	1			
	0			
Cognitive Symptoms / Brain Fog	3			
	2			
	1			
	0			

		Morning	Afternoon	Evening
Anxiety / Low Mood	3			
	2			
	1			
	0			
Activity Levels	3			
	2			
	1			
	0			
Other	3			
	2			
	1			
	0			

Symptom Score: 0 = No problem, 1 = Slight, 2 = Moderate, 3 = Severe. See p.3

Today's Notes:

Pain Location & Levels

Shade bodies, tick boxes or use pain score.

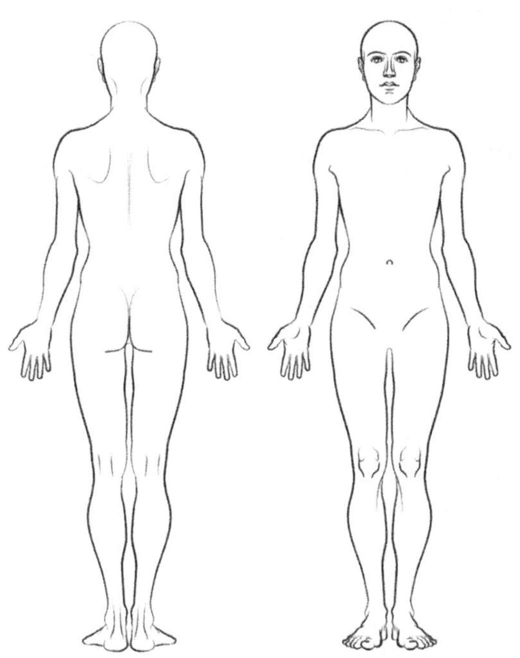

Pain Score
1 = Slight, 2 = Moderate, 3 = Severe.

	Left	Right
Jaw		
Neck		
Shoulder Girdle		
Chest		
Upper Back		
Lower Back		
Upper Arm		
Lower Arm		
Abdomen		
Hip / Buttock		
Upper Leg		
Lower Leg		

Notes

Today I Experienced			
Headache / Migraine		Diarrhoea	
Muscle Twinges / Cramps		Constipation	
Muscle Weakness		Bloating / Stomach Pain / IBS	
Skin Itching / Burning / Hives / Rash (circle all that apply)		Bladder Issues	
Bruising		Swelling	
Sweating		Stress	
Nervousness		Nausea / vomiting	
Sensitive to Sensory Stimulation (light / noise / temperature)		Numbness / Tingling (name part of body)	
Dizziness		Missed meal / unusual food	
Loss of appetite		Hormonal Changes	
Other:		Other:	
Other:		Other:	

Date: ***Weather:***

Hours Slept: Insomnia? Yes ☐ No ☐

How did you feel on waking today? I felt refreshed: ☐

Slightly unrefreshed: ☐ Moderately unrefreshed: ☐ Severely unrefreshed: ☐

Did you exercise today? Yes ☐ No ☐

		Morning	Afternoon	Evening
Fatigue	3			
	2			
	1			
	0			
Pain Levels	3			
	2			
	1			
	0			
Cognitive Symptoms / Brain Fog	3			
	2			
	1			
	0			

		Morning	Afternoon	Evening
Anxiety / Low Mood	3			
	2			
	1			
	0			
Activity Levels	3			
	2			
	1			
	0			
Other	3			
	2			
	1			
	0			

Symptom Score: 0 = No problem, 1 = Slight, 2 = Moderate, 3 = Severe. See p.3

Today's Notes:

Pain Location & Levels

Shade bodies, tick boxes or use pain score.

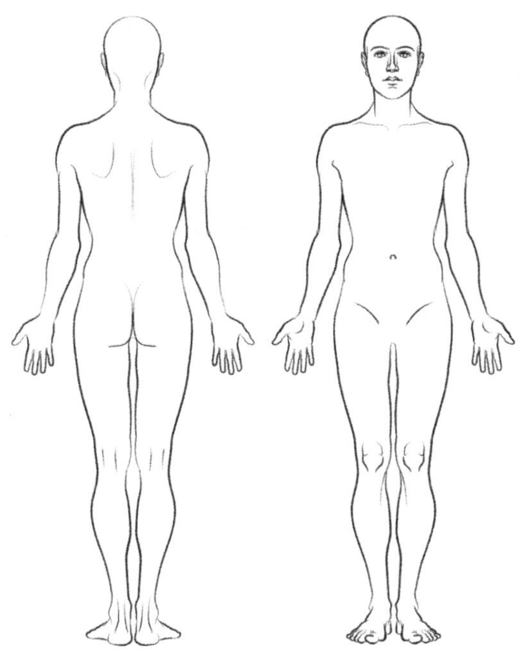

Pain Score
1 = Slight, 2 = Moderate, 3 = Severe.

	Left	Right
Jaw		
Neck		
Shoulder Girdle		
Chest		
Upper Back		
Lower Back		
Upper Arm		
Lower Arm		
Abdomen		
Hip / Buttock		
Upper Leg		
Lower Leg		

Notes

Today I Experienced			
Headache / Migraine		Diarrhoea	
Muscle Twinges / Cramps		Constipation	
Muscle Weakness		Bloating / Stomach Pain / IBS	
Skin Itching / Burning / Hives / Rash (circle all that apply)		Bladder Issues	
Bruising		Swelling	
Sweating		Stress	
Nervousness		Nausea / vomiting	
Sensitive to Sensory Stimulation (light / noise / temperature)		Numbness / Tingling (name part of body)	
Dizziness		Missed meal / unusual food	
Loss of appetite		Hormonal Changes	
Other:		Other:	
Other:		Other:	

Date: ***Weather:***

Hours Slept: Insomnia? Yes ☐ No ☐

How did you feel on waking today? I felt refreshed: ☐

Slightly unrefreshed: ☐ Moderately unrefreshed: ☐ Severely unrefreshed: ☐

Did you exercise today? Yes ☐ No ☐

		Morning	Afternoon	Evening
	3			
	2			
	1			
Fatigue	0			
	3			
	2			
	1			
Pain Levels	0			
	3			
	2			
	1			
Cognitive Symptoms / Brain Fog	0			

		Morning	Afternoon	Evening
	3			
	2			
	1			
Anxiety / Low Mood	0			
	3			
	2			
	1			
Activity Levels	0			
	3			
	2			
	1			
Other	0			

Symptom Score: 0 = No problem, 1 = Slight, 2 = Moderate, 3 = Severe. See p.3

Today's Notes:

Pain Location & Levels

Shade bodies, tick boxes or use pain score.

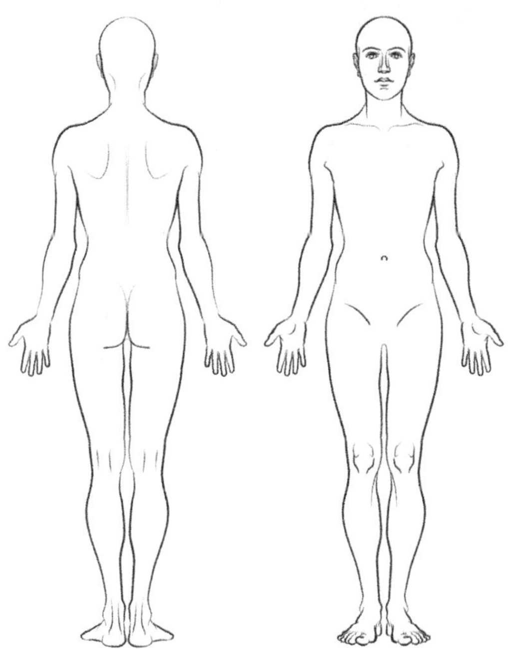

Pain Score
1 = Slight, 2 = Moderate, 3 = Severe.

	Left	Right
Jaw		
Neck		
Shoulder Girdle		
Chest		
Upper Back		
Lower Back		
Upper Arm		
Lower Arm		
Abdomen		
Hip / Buttock		
Upper Leg		
Lower Leg		

Notes

Today I Experienced			
Headache / Migraine		Diarrhoea	
Muscle Twinges / Cramps		Constipation	
Muscle Weakness		Bloating / Stomach Pain / IBS	
Skin Itching / Burning / Hives / Rash (circle all that apply)		Bladder Issues	
Bruising		Swelling	
Sweating		Stress	
Nervousness		Nausea / vomiting	
Sensitive to Sensory Stimulation (light / noise / temperature)		Numbness / Tingling (name part of body)	
Dizziness		Missed meal / unusual food	
Loss of appetite		Hormonal Changes	
Other:		Other:	
Other:		Other:	

Date: ***Weather:***

Hours Slept: Insomnia? Yes ☐ No ☐

How did you feel on waking today? I felt refreshed: ☐

Slightly unrefreshed: ☐ Moderately unrefreshed: ☐ Severely unrefreshed: ☐

Did you exercise today? Yes ☐ No ☐

		Morning	Afternoon	Evening
Fatigue	3			
	2			
	1			
	0			
Pain Levels	3			
	2			
	1			
	0			
Cognitive Symptoms / Brain Fog	3			
	2			
	1			
	0			

		Morning	Afternoon	Evening
Anxiety / Low Mood	3			
	2			
	1			
	0			
Activity Levels	3			
	2			
	1			
	0			
Other	3			
	2			
	1			
	0			

Symptom Score: 0 = No problem, 1 = Slight, 2 = Moderate, 3 = Severe. See p.3

Today's Notes:

Pain Location & Levels

Shade bodies, tick boxes or use pain score.

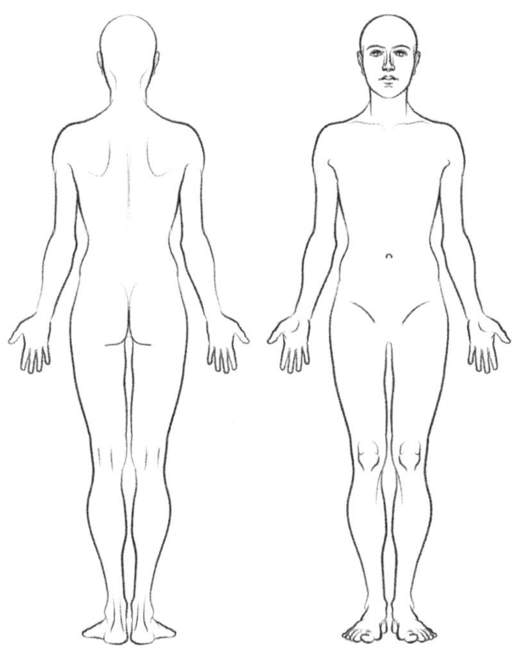

Pain Score
1 = Slight, 2 = Moderate, 3 = Severe.

	Left	Right
Jaw		
Neck		
Shoulder Girdle		
Chest		
Upper Back		
Lower Back		
Upper Arm		
Lower Arm		
Abdomen		
Hip / Buttock		
Upper Leg		
Lower Leg		

Notes

Today I Experienced			
Headache / Migraine		Diarrhoea	
Muscle Twinges / Cramps		Constipation	
Muscle Weakness		Bloating / Stomach Pain / IBS	
Skin Itching / Burning / Hives / Rash (circle all that apply)		Bladder Issues	
Bruising		Swelling	
Sweating		Stress	
Nervousness		Nausea / vomiting	
Sensitive to Sensory Stimulation (light / noise / temperature)		Numbness / Tingling (name part of body)	
Dizziness		Missed meal / unusual food	
Loss of appetite		Hormonal Changes	
Other:		Other:	
Other:		Other:	

Date: ***Weather:***

Hours Slept: Insomnia? Yes ☐ No ☐

How did you feel on waking today? I felt refreshed: ☐

Slightly unrefreshed: ☐ Moderately unrefreshed: ☐ Severely unrefreshed: ☐

Did you exercise today? Yes ☐ No ☐

		Morning	Afternoon	Evening
	3			
	2			
	1			
Fatigue	0			
	3			
	2			
	1			
Pain Levels	0			
	3			
Cognitive Symptoms / Brain Fog	2			
	1			
	0			

		Morning	Afternoon	Evening
	3			
	2			
	1			
Anxiety / Low Mood	0			
	3			
	2			
	1			
Activity Levels	0			
	3			
	2			
	1			
Other	0			

Symptom Score: 0 = No problem, 1 = Slight, 2 = Moderate, 3 = Severe. See p.3

Today's Notes:

Pain Location & Levels

Shade bodies, tick boxes or use pain score.

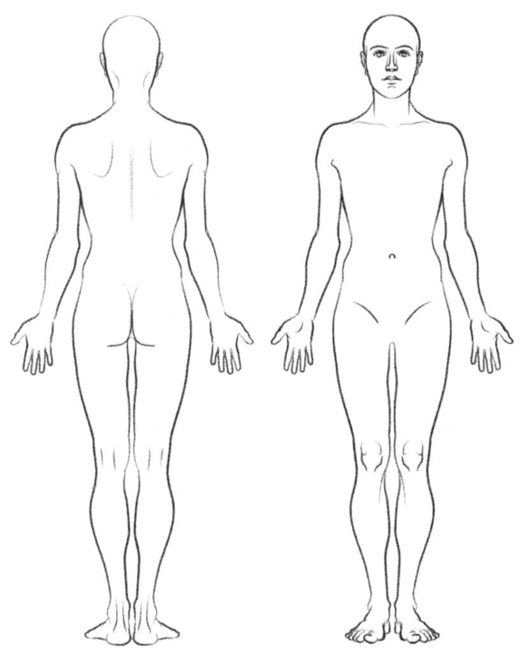

Pain Score
1 = Slight, 2 = Moderate, 3 = Severe.

	Left	Right
Jaw		
Neck		
Shoulder Girdle		
Chest		
Upper Back		
Lower Back		
Upper Arm		
Lower Arm		
Abdomen		
Hip / Buttock		
Upper Leg		
Lower Leg		

Notes

Today I Experienced			
Headache / Migraine		Diarrhoea	
Muscle Twinges / Cramps		Constipation	
Muscle Weakness		Bloating / Stomach Pain / IBS	
Skin Itching / Burning / Hives / Rash (circle all that apply)		Bladder Issues	
Bruising		Swelling	
Sweating		Stress	
Nervousness		Nausea / vomiting	
Sensitive to Sensory Stimulation (light / noise / temperature)		Numbness / Tingling (name part of body)	
Dizziness		Missed meal / unusual food	
Loss of appetite		Hormonal Changes	
Other:		Other:	
Other:		Other:	

Date: ***Weather:***

Hours Slept: Insomnia? Yes ☐ No ☐

How did you feel on waking today? I felt refreshed: ☐

Slightly unrefreshed: ☐ Moderately unrefreshed: ☐ Severely unrefreshed: ☐

Did you exercise today? Yes ☐ No ☐

		Morning	Afternoon	Evening
Fatigue	3			
	2			
	1			
	0			
Pain Levels	3			
	2			
	1			
	0			
Cognitive Symptoms / Brain Fog	3			
	2			
	1			
	0			

		Morning	Afternoon	Evening
Anxiety / Low Mood	3			
	2			
	1			
	0			
Activity Levels	3			
	2			
	1			
	0			
Other	3			
	2			
	1			
	0			

Symptom Score: 0 = No problem, 1 = Slight, 2 = Moderate, 3 = Severe. See p.3

Today's Notes:

Pain Location & Levels

Shade bodies, tick boxes or use pain score.

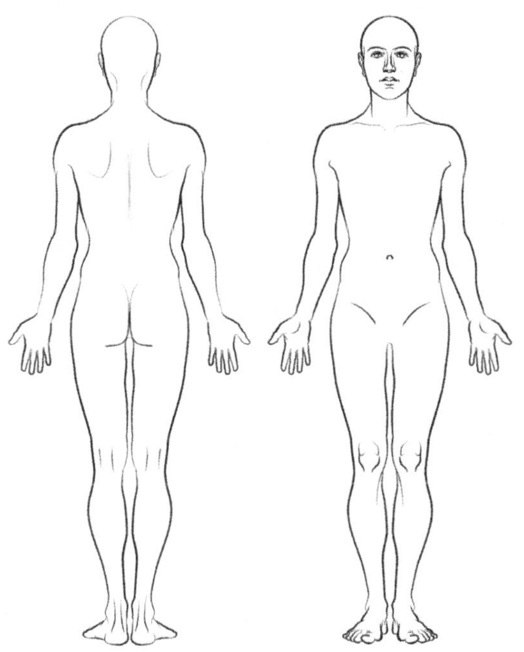

Pain Score
1 = Slight, 2 = Moderate, 3 = Severe.

	Left	Right
Jaw		
Neck		
Shoulder Girdle		
Chest		
Upper Back		
Lower Back		
Upper Arm		
Lower Arm		
Abdomen		
Hip / Buttock		
Upper Leg		
Lower Leg		

Notes

Today I Experienced			
Headache / Migraine		Diarrhoea	
Muscle Twinges / Cramps		Constipation	
Muscle Weakness		Bloating / Stomach Pain / IBS	
Skin Itching / Burning / Hives / Rash (circle all that apply)		Bladder Issues	
Bruising		Swelling	
Sweating		Stress	
Nervousness		Nausea / vomiting	
Sensitive to Sensory Stimulation (light / noise / temperature)		Numbness / Tingling (name part of body)	
Dizziness		Missed meal / unusual food	
Loss of appetite		Hormonal Changes	
Other:		Other:	
Other:		Other:	

Date: **Weather:**

Hours Slept: Insomnia? Yes ☐ No ☐

How did you feel on waking today? I felt refreshed: ☐

Slightly unrefreshed: ☐ Moderately unrefreshed: ☐ Severely unrefreshed: ☐

Did you exercise today? Yes ☐ No ☐

		Morning	Afternoon	Evening
Fatigue	3			
	2			
	1			
	0			
Pain Levels	3			
	2			
	1			
	0			
Cognitive Symptoms / Brain Fog	3			
	2			
	1			
	0			

		Morning	Afternoon	Evening
Anxiety / Low Mood	3			
	2			
	1			
	0			
Activity Levels	3			
	2			
	1			
	0			
Other	3			
	2			
	1			
	0			

Symptom Score: 0 = No problem, 1 = Slight, 2 = Moderate, 3 = Severe. See p.3

Today's Notes:

Pain Location & Levels

Shade bodies, tick boxes or use pain score.

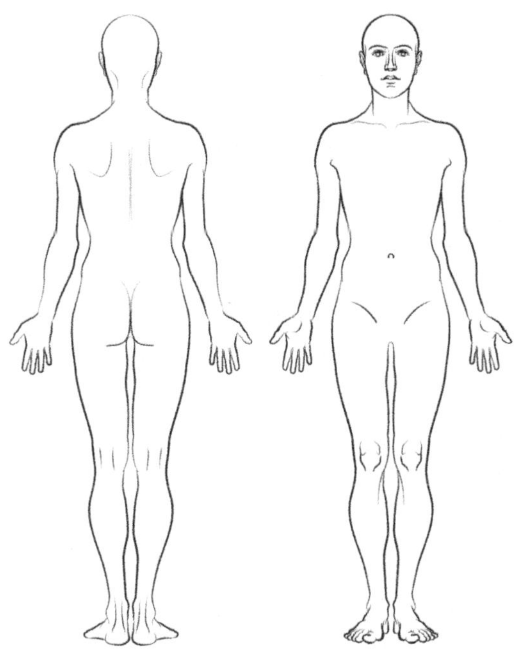

Pain Score

1 = Slight, 2 = Moderate, 3 = Severe.

	Left	Right
Jaw		
Neck		
Shoulder Girdle		
Chest		
Upper Back		
Lower Back		
Upper Arm		
Lower Arm		
Abdomen		
Hip / Buttock		
Upper Leg		
Lower Leg		

Notes

Today I Experienced			
Headache / Migraine		Diarrhoea	
Muscle Twinges / Cramps		Constipation	
Muscle Weakness		Bloating / Stomach Pain / IBS	
Skin Itching / Burning / Hives / Rash (circle all that apply)		Bladder Issues	
Bruising		Swelling	
Sweating		Stress	
Nervousness		Nausea / vomiting	
Sensitive to Sensory Stimulation (light / noise / temperature)		Numbness / Tingling (name part of body)	
Dizziness		Missed meal / unusual food	
Loss of appetite		Hormonal Changes	
Other:		Other:	
Other:		Other:	

Date: ________ ***Weather:*** ________

Hours Slept: ________ Insomnia? Yes ☐ No ☐

How did you feel on waking today? I felt refreshed: ☐

Slightly unrefreshed: ☐ Moderately unrefreshed: ☐ Severely unrefreshed: ☐

Did you exercise today? Yes ☐ No ☐ ________

		Morning	Afternoon	Evening
Fatigue	3			
	2			
	1			
	0			
Pain Levels	3			
	2			
	1			
	0			
Cognitive Symptoms / Brain Fog	3			
	2			
	1			
	0			

		Morning	Afternoon	Evening
Anxiety / Low Mood	3			
	2			
	1			
	0			
Activity Levels	3			
	2			
	1			
	0			
Other	3			
	2			
	1			
	0			

Symptom Score: 0 = No problem, 1 = Slight, 2 = Moderate, 3 = Severe. See p.3

Today's Notes:

Pain Location & Levels

Shade bodies, tick boxes or use pain score.

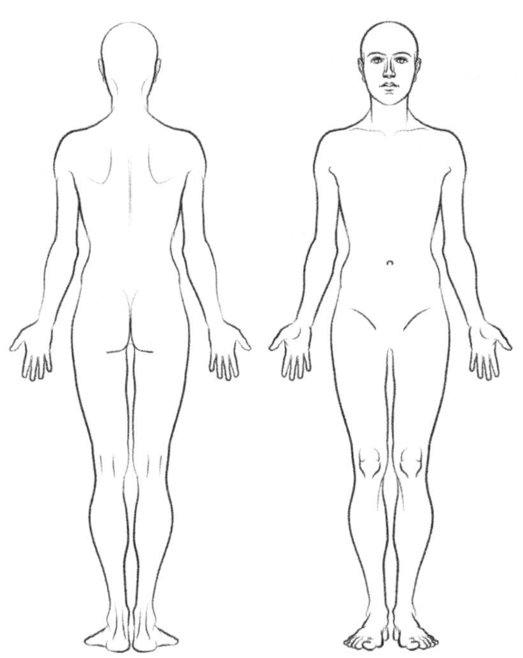

Pain Score
1 = Slight, 2 = Moderate, 3 = Severe.

	Left	Right
Jaw		
Neck		
Shoulder Girdle		
Chest		
Upper Back		
Lower Back		
Upper Arm		
Lower Arm		
Abdomen		
Hip / Buttock		
Upper Leg		
Lower Leg		

Notes

Today I Experienced			
Headache / Migraine		Diarrhoea	
Muscle Twinges / Cramps		Constipation	
Muscle Weakness		Bloating / Stomach Pain / IBS	
Skin Itching / Burning / Hives / Rash (circle all that apply)		Bladder Issues	
Bruising		Swelling	
Sweating		Stress	
Nervousness		Nausea / vomiting	
Sensitive to Sensory Stimulation (light / noise / temperature)		Numbness / Tingling (name part of body)	
Dizziness		Missed meal / unusual food	
Loss of appetite		Hormonal Changes	
Other:		Other:	
Other:		Other:	

Date: ***Weather:***

Hours Slept: Insomnia? Yes ☐ No ☐

How did you feel on waking today? I felt refreshed: ☐

Slightly unrefreshed: ☐ Moderately unrefreshed: ☐ Severely unrefreshed: ☐

Did you exercise today? Yes ☐ No ☐

		Morning	Afternoon	Evening
	3			
	2			
	1			
Fatigue	0			
	3			
	2			
	1			
Pain Levels	0			
	3			
Cognitive Symptoms / Brain Fog	2			
	1			
	0			

		Morning	Afternoon	Evening
	3			
	2			
Anxiety / Low Mood	1			
	0			
	3			
	2			
	1			
Activity Levels	0			
	3			
	2			
	1			
Other	0			

Symptom Score: 0 = No problem, 1 = Slight, 2 = Moderate, 3 = Severe. See p.3

Today's Notes:

Pain Location & Levels

Shade bodies, tick boxes or use pain score.

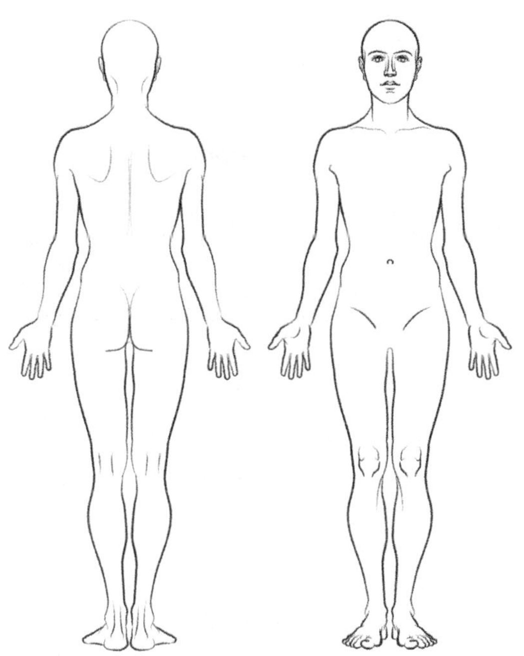

Pain Score
1 = Slight, 2 = Moderate, 3 = Severe.

	Left	Right
Jaw		
Neck		
Shoulder Girdle		
Chest		
Upper Back		
Lower Back		
Upper Arm		
Lower Arm		
Abdomen		
Hip / Buttock		
Upper Leg		
Lower Leg		

Notes

Today I Experienced			
Headache / Migraine		Diarrhoea	
Muscle Twinges / Cramps		Constipation	
Muscle Weakness		Bloating / Stomach Pain / IBS	
Skin Itching / Burning / Hives / Rash (circle all that apply)		Bladder Issues	
Bruising		Swelling	
Sweating		Stress	
Nervousness		Nausea / vomiting	
Sensitive to Sensory Stimulation (light / noise / temperature)		Numbness / Tingling (name part of body)	
Dizziness		Missed meal / unusual food	
Loss of appetite		Hormonal Changes	
Other:		Other:	
Other:		Other:	

Date: ***Weather:***

Hours Slept: Insomnia? Yes ☐ No ☐

How did you feel on waking today? I felt refreshed: ☐

Slightly unrefreshed: ☐ Moderately unrefreshed: ☐ Severely unrefreshed: ☐

Did you exercise today? Yes ☐ No ☐

		Morning	Afternoon	Evening
	3			
	2			
	1			
Fatigue	0			
	3			
	2			
	1			
Pain Levels	0			
	3			
	2			
	1			
Cognitive Symptoms / Brain Fog	0			

		Morning	Afternoon	Evening
	3			
	2			
	1			
Anxiety / Low Mood	0			
	3			
	2			
	1			
Activity Levels	0			
	3			
	2			
	1			
Other	0			

Symptom Score: 0 = No problem, 1 = Slight, 2 = Moderate, 3 = Severe. See p.3

Today's Notes:

Pain Location & Levels

Shade bodies, tick boxes or use pain score.

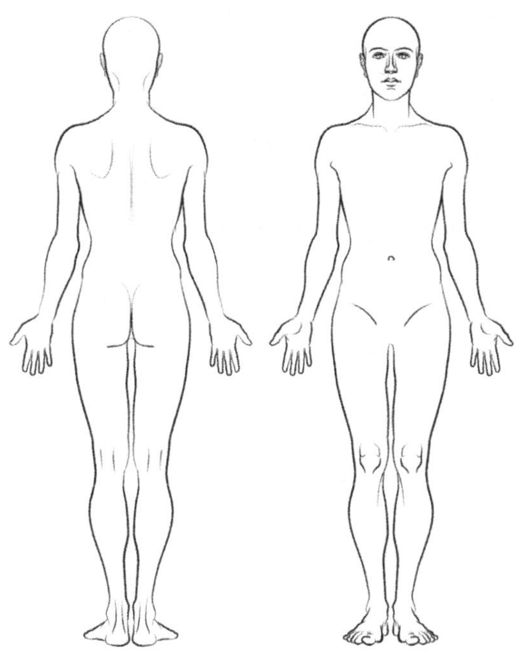

Pain Score
1 = Slight, 2 = Moderate, 3 = Severe.

	Left	Right
Jaw		
Neck		
Shoulder Girdle		
Chest		
Upper Back		
Lower Back		
Upper Arm		
Lower Arm		
Abdomen		
Hip / Buttock		
Upper Leg		
Lower Leg		

Notes

Today I Experienced			
Headache / Migraine		Diarrhoea	
Muscle Twinges / Cramps		Constipation	
Muscle Weakness		Bloating / Stomach Pain / IBS	
Skin Itching / Burning / Hives / Rash (circle all that apply)		Bladder Issues	
Bruising		Swelling	
Sweating		Stress	
Nervousness		Nausea / vomiting	
Sensitive to Sensory Stimulation (light / noise / temperature)		Numbness / Tingling (name part of body)	
Dizziness		Missed meal / unusual food	
Loss of appetite		Hormonal Changes	
Other:		Other:	
Other:		Other:	

Date: ***Weather:***

Hours Slept: Insomnia? Yes ☐ No ☐

How did you feel on waking today? I felt refreshed: ☐

Slightly unrefreshed: ☐ Moderately unrefreshed: ☐ Severely unrefreshed: ☐

Did you exercise today? Yes ☐ No ☐

		Morning	Afternoon	Evening
Fatigue	3			
	2			
	1			
	0			
Pain Levels	3			
	2			
	1			
	0			
Cognitive Symptoms / Brain Fog	3			
	2			
	1			
	0			

		Morning	Afternoon	Evening
Anxiety / Low Mood	3			
	2			
	1			
	0			
Activity Levels	3			
	2			
	1			
	0			
Other	3			
	2			
	1			
	0			

Symptom Score: 0 = No problem, 1 = Slight, 2 = Moderate, 3 = Severe. See p.3

Today's Notes:

Pain Location & Levels

Shade bodies, tick boxes or use pain score.

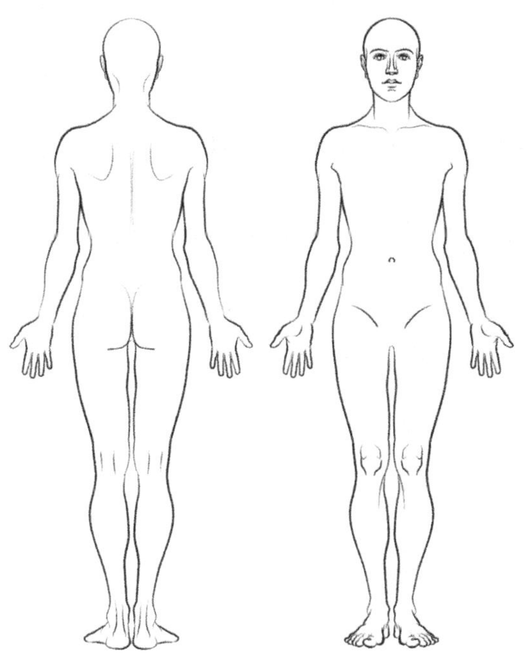

Pain Score
1 = Slight, 2 = Moderate, 3 = Severe.

	Left	Right
Jaw		
Neck		
Shoulder Girdle		
Chest		
Upper Back		
Lower Back		
Upper Arm		
Lower Arm		
Abdomen		
Hip / Buttock		
Upper Leg		
Lower Leg		

Notes

Today I Experienced			
Headache / Migraine		Diarrhoea	
Muscle Twinges / Cramps		Constipation	
Muscle Weakness		Bloating / Stomach Pain / IBS	
Skin Itching / Burning / Hives / Rash (circle all that apply)		Bladder Issues	
Bruising		Swelling	
Sweating		Stress	
Nervousness		Nausea / vomiting	
Sensitive to Sensory Stimulation (light / noise / temperature)		Numbness / Tingling (name part of body)	
Dizziness		Missed meal / unusual food	
Loss of appetite		Hormonal Changes	
Other:		Other:	
Other:		Other:	

Date: ***Weather:***

Hours Slept: Insomnia? Yes ☐ No ☐

How did you feel on waking today? I felt refreshed: ☐

Slightly unrefreshed: ☐ Moderately unrefreshed: ☐ Severely unrefreshed: ☐

Did you exercise today? Yes ☐ No ☐

		Morning	Afternoon	Evening
Fatigue	3			
	2			
	1			
	0			
Pain Levels	3			
	2			
	1			
	0			
Cognitive Symptoms / Brain Fog	3			
	2			
	1			
	0			

		Morning	Afternoon	Evening
Anxiety / Low Mood	3			
	2			
	1			
	0			
Activity Levels	3			
	2			
	1			
	0			
Other	3			
	2			
	1			
	0			

Symptom Score: 0 = No problem, 1 = Slight, 2 = Moderate, 3 = Severe. See p.3

Today's Notes:

Pain Location & Levels

Shade bodies, tick boxes or use pain score.

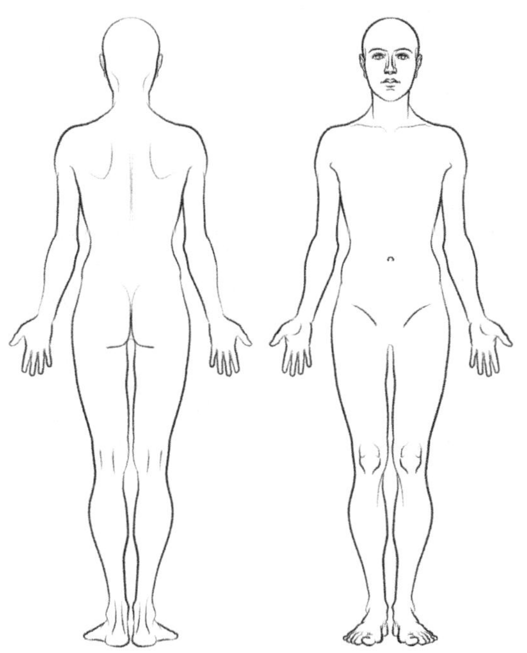

Pain Score
1 = Slight, 2 = Moderate, 3 = Severe.

	Left	Right
Jaw		
Neck		
Shoulder Girdle		
Chest		
Upper Back		
Lower Back		
Upper Arm		
Lower Arm		
Abdomen		
Hip / Buttock		
Upper Leg		
Lower Leg		

Notes

Today I Experienced			
Headache / Migraine		Diarrhoea	
Muscle Twinges / Cramps		Constipation	
Muscle Weakness		Bloating / Stomach Pain / IBS	
Skin Itching / Burning / Hives / Rash (circle all that apply)		Bladder Issues	
Bruising		Swelling	
Sweating		Stress	
Nervousness		Nausea / vomiting	
Sensitive to Sensory Stimulation (light / noise / temperature)		Numbness / Tingling (name part of body)	
Dizziness		Missed meal / unusual food	
Loss of appetite		Hormonal Changes	
Other:		Other:	
Other:		Other:	

Date: ***Weather:***

Hours Slept: Insomnia? Yes ☐ No ☐

How did you feel on waking today? I felt refreshed: ☐

Slightly unrefreshed: ☐ Moderately unrefreshed: ☐ Severely unrefreshed: ☐

Did you exercise today? Yes ☐ No ☐

		Morning	Afternoon	Evening
Fatigue	3			
	2			
	1			
	0			
Pain Levels	3			
	2			
	1			
	0			
Cognitive Symptoms / Brain Fog	3			
	2			
	1			
	0			

		Morning	Afternoon	Evening
Anxiety / Low Mood	3			
	2			
	1			
	0			
Activity Levels	3			
	2			
	1			
	0			
Other	3			
	2			
	1			
	0			

Symptom Score: 0 = No problem, 1 = Slight, 2 = Moderate, 3 = Severe. See p.3

Today's Notes:

Pain Location & Levels

Shade bodies, tick boxes or use pain score.

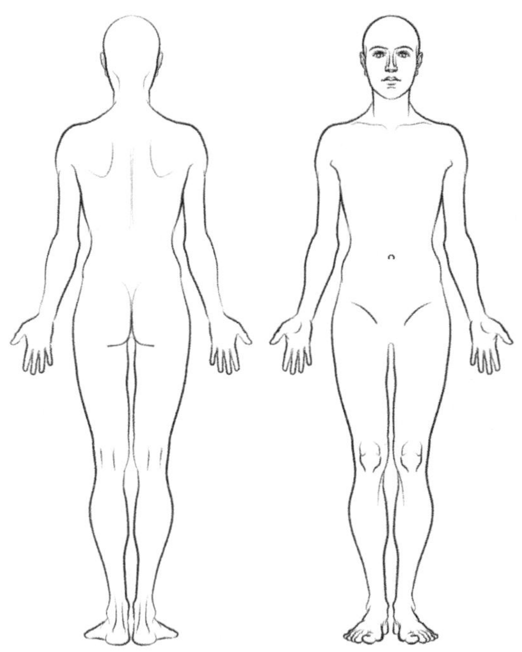

Pain Score
1 = Slight, 2 = Moderate, 3 = Severe.

	Left	Right
Jaw		
Neck		
Shoulder Girdle		
Chest		
Upper Back		
Lower Back		
Upper Arm		
Lower Arm		
Abdomen		
Hip / Buttock		
Upper Leg		
Lower Leg		

Notes

Today I Experienced			
Headache / Migraine		Diarrhoea	
Muscle Twinges / Cramps		Constipation	
Muscle Weakness		Bloating / Stomach Pain / IBS	
Skin Itching / Burning / Hives / Rash (circle all that apply)		Bladder Issues	
Bruising		Swelling	
Sweating		Stress	
Nervousness		Nausea / vomiting	
Sensitive to Sensory Stimulation (light / noise / temperature)		Numbness / Tingling (name part of body)	
Dizziness		Missed meal / unusual food	
Loss of appetite		Hormonal Changes	
Other:		Other:	
Other:		Other:	

Date: ***Weather:***

Hours Slept: Insomnia? Yes ☐ No ☐

How did you feel on waking today? I felt refreshed: ☐

Slightly unrefreshed: ☐ Moderately unrefreshed: ☐ Severely unrefreshed: ☐

Did you exercise today? Yes ☐ No ☐

		Morning	Afternoon	Evening
Fatigue	3			
	2			
	1			
	0			
Pain Levels	3			
	2			
	1			
	0			
Cognitive Symptoms / Brain Fog	3			
	2			
	1			
	0			

		Morning	Afternoon	Evening
Anxiety / Low Mood	3			
	2			
	1			
	0			
Activity Levels	3			
	2			
	1			
	0			
Other	3			
	2			
	1			
	0			

Symptom Score: 0 = No problem, 1 = Slight, 2 = Moderate, 3 = Severe. See p.3

Today's Notes:

Pain Location & Levels

Shade bodies, tick boxes or use pain score.

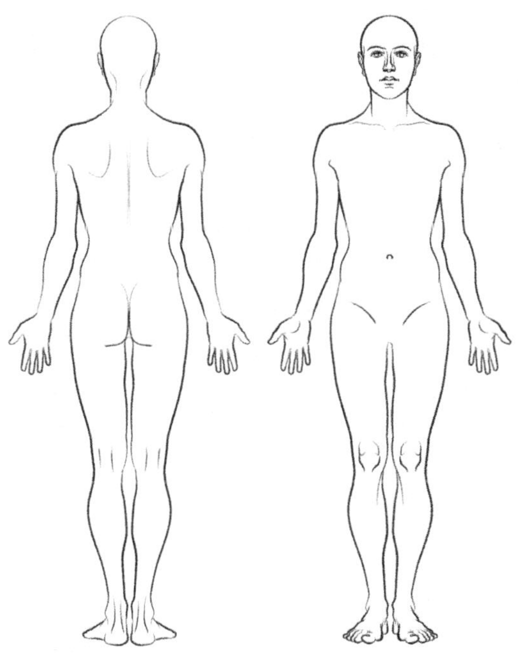

Pain Score
1 = Slight, 2 = Moderate, 3 = Severe.

	Left	Right
Jaw		
Neck		
Shoulder Girdle		
Chest		
Upper Back		
Lower Back		
Upper Arm		
Lower Arm		
Abdomen		
Hip / Buttock		
Upper Leg		
Lower Leg		

Notes

Today I Experienced			
Headache / Migraine		Diarrhoea	
Muscle Twinges / Cramps		Constipation	
Muscle Weakness		Bloating / Stomach Pain / IBS	
Skin Itching / Burning / Hives / Rash (circle all that apply)		Bladder Issues	
Bruising		Swelling	
Sweating		Stress	
Nervousness		Nausea / vomiting	
Sensitive to Sensory Stimulation (light / noise / temperature)		Numbness / Tingling (name part of body)	
Dizziness		Missed meal / unusual food	
Loss of appetite		Hormonal Changes	
Other:		Other:	
Other:		Other:	

Date: ***Weather:***

Hours Slept: Insomnia? Yes ☐ No ☐

How did you feel on waking today? I felt refreshed: ☐

Slightly unrefreshed: ☐ Moderately unrefreshed: ☐ Severely unrefreshed: ☐

Did you exercise today? Yes ☐ No ☐

		Morning	Afternoon	Evening
Fatigue	3			
	2			
	1			
	0			
Pain Levels	3			
	2			
	1			
	0			
Cognitive Symptoms / Brain Fog	3			
	2			
	1			
	0			

		Morning	Afternoon	Evening
Anxiety / Low Mood	3			
	2			
	1			
	0			
Activity Levels	3			
	2			
	1			
	0			
Other	3			
	2			
	1			
	0			

Symptom Score: 0 = No problem, 1 = Slight, 2 = Moderate, 3 = Severe. See p.3

Today's Notes:

Pain Location & Levels

Shade bodies, tick boxes or use pain score.

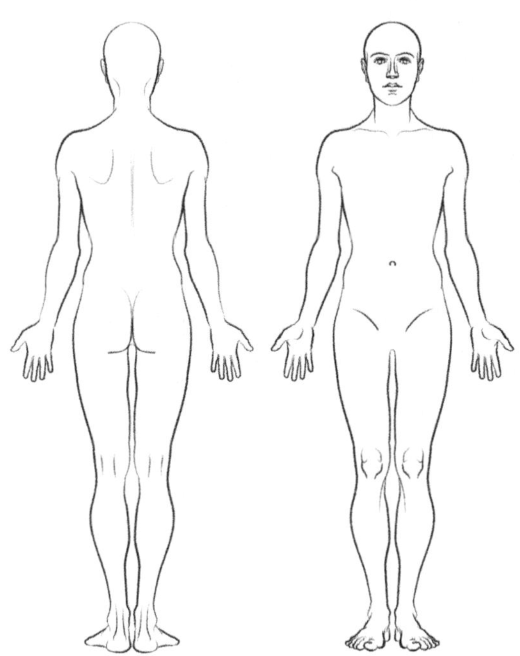

Pain Score
1 = Slight, 2 = Moderate, 3 = Severe.

	Left	Right
Jaw		
Neck		
Shoulder Girdle		
Chest		
Upper Back		
Lower Back		
Upper Arm		
Lower Arm		
Abdomen		
Hip / Buttock		
Upper Leg		
Lower Leg		

Notes

Today I Experienced			
Headache / Migraine		Diarrhoea	
Muscle Twinges / Cramps		Constipation	
Muscle Weakness		Bloating / Stomach Pain / IBS	
Skin Itching / Burning / Hives / Rash (circle all that apply)		Bladder Issues	
Bruising		Swelling	
Sweating		Stress	
Nervousness		Nausea / vomiting	
Sensitive to Sensory Stimulation (light / noise / temperature)		Numbness / Tingling (name part of body)	
Dizziness		Missed meal / unusual food	
Loss of appetite		Hormonal Changes	
Other:		Other:	
Other:		Other:	

Date: ***Weather:***

Hours Slept: Insomnia? Yes ☐ No ☐

How did you feel on waking today? I felt refreshed: ☐

Slightly unrefreshed: ☐ Moderately unrefreshed: ☐ Severely unrefreshed: ☐

Did you exercise today? Yes ☐ No ☐

		Morning	Afternoon	Evening
Fatigue	3			
	2			
	1			
	0			
Pain Levels	3			
	2			
	1			
	0			
Cognitive Symptoms / Brain Fog	3			
	2			
	1			
	0			

		Morning	Afternoon	Evening
Anxiety / Low Mood	3			
	2			
	1			
	0			
Activity Levels	3			
	2			
	1			
	0			
Other	3			
	2			
	1			
	0			

Symptom Score: 0 = No problem, 1 = Slight, 2 = Moderate, 3 = Severe. See p.3

Today's Notes:

Pain Location & Levels

Shade bodies, tick boxes or use pain score.

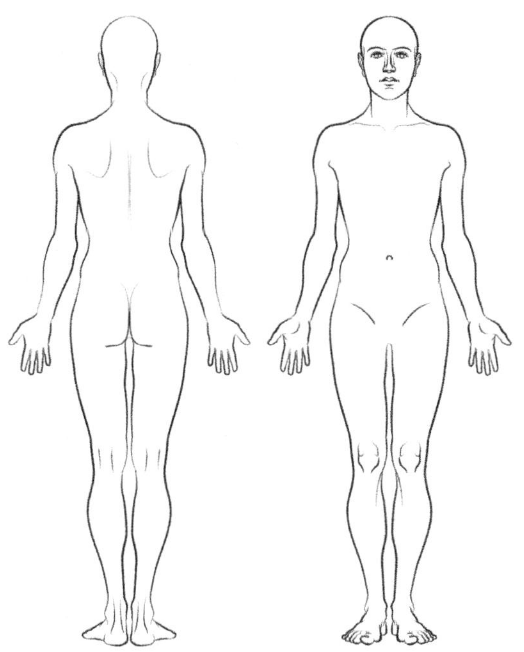

Pain Score
1 = Slight, 2 = Moderate, 3 = Severe.

	Left	Right
Jaw		
Neck		
Shoulder Girdle		
Chest		
Upper Back		
Lower Back		
Upper Arm		
Lower Arm		
Abdomen		
Hip / Buttock		
Upper Leg		
Lower Leg		

Notes

Today I Experienced			
Headache / Migraine		Diarrhoea	
Muscle Twinges / Cramps		Constipation	
Muscle Weakness		Bloating / Stomach Pain / IBS	
Skin Itching / Burning / Hives / Rash (circle all that apply)		Bladder Issues	
Bruising		Swelling	
Sweating		Stress	
Nervousness		Nausea / vomiting	
Sensitive to Sensory Stimulation (light / noise / temperature)		Numbness / Tingling (name part of body)	
Dizziness		Missed meal / unusual food	
Loss of appetite		Hormonal Changes	
Other:		Other:	
Other:		Other:	

Date: ***Weather:***

Hours Slept: Insomnia? Yes ☐ No ☐

How did you feel on waking today? I felt refreshed: ☐

Slightly unrefreshed: ☐ Moderately unrefreshed: ☐ Severely unrefreshed: ☐

Did you exercise today? Yes ☐ No ☐

		Morning	Afternoon	Evening
	3			
	2			
	1			
Fatigue	0			
	3			
	2			
	1			
Pain Levels	0			
	3			
	2			
	1			
Cognitive Symptoms / Brain Fog	0			

		Morning	Afternoon	Evening
	3			
	2			
	1			
Anxiety / Low Mood	0			
	3			
	2			
	1			
Activity Levels	0			
	3			
	2			
	1			
Other	0			

Symptom Score: 0 = No problem, 1 = Slight, 2 = Moderate, 3 = Severe. See p.3

Today's Notes:

Pain Location & Levels

Shade bodies, tick boxes or use pain score.

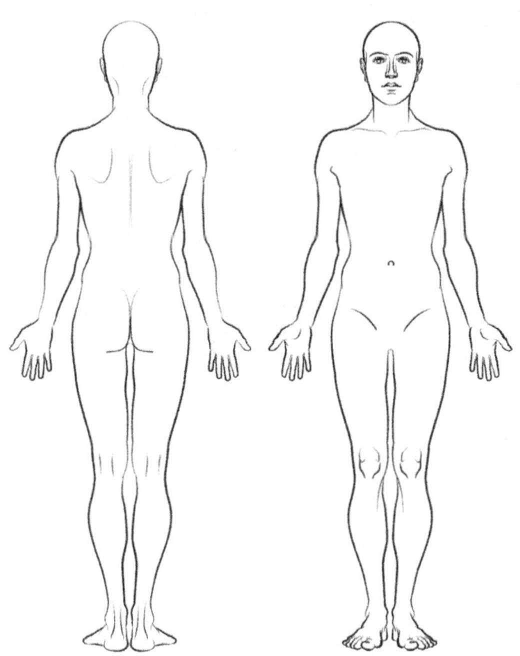

Pain Score
1 = Slight, 2 = Moderate, 3 = Severe.

	Left	Right
Jaw		
Neck		
Shoulder Girdle		
Chest		
Upper Back		
Lower Back		
Upper Arm		
Lower Arm		
Abdomen		
Hip / Buttock		
Upper Leg		
Lower Leg		

Notes

Today I Experienced			
Headache / Migraine		Diarrhoea	
Muscle Twinges / Cramps		Constipation	
Muscle Weakness		Bloating / Stomach Pain / IBS	
Skin Itching / Burning / Hives / Rash (circle all that apply)		Bladder Issues	
Bruising		Swelling	
Sweating		Stress	
Nervousness		Nausea / vomiting	
Sensitive to Sensory Stimulation (light / noise / temperature)		Numbness / Tingling (name part of body)	
Dizziness		Missed meal / unusual food	
Loss of appetite		Hormonal Changes	
Other:		Other:	
Other:		Other:	

Date: ________________ ***Weather:*** ________________

Hours Slept: ________________ Insomnia? Yes ☐ No ☐

How did you feel on waking today? I felt refreshed: ☐

Slightly unrefreshed: ☐ Moderately unrefreshed: ☐ Severely unrefreshed: ☐

Did you exercise today? Yes ☐ No ☐ ________________

		Morning	Afternoon	Evening
Fatigue	3			
	2			
	1			
	0			
Pain Levels	3			
	2			
	1			
	0			
Cognitive Symptoms / Brain Fog	3			
	2			
	1			
	0			

		Morning	Afternoon	Evening
Anxiety / Low Mood	3			
	2			
	1			
	0			
Activity Levels	3			
	2			
	1			
	0			
Other	3			
	2			
	1			
	0			

Symptom Score: 0 = No problem, 1 = Slight, 2 = Moderate, 3 = Severe. See p.3

Today's Notes:

Pain Location & Levels

Shade bodies, tick boxes or use pain score.

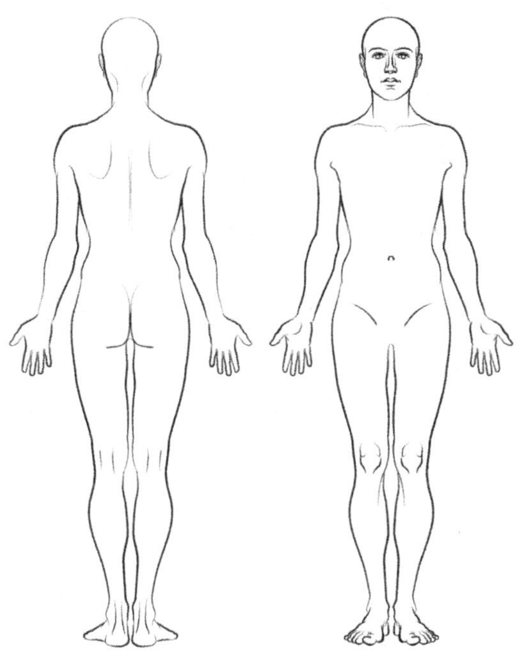

Pain Score
1 = Slight, 2 = Moderate, 3 = Severe.

	Left	Right
Jaw		
Neck		
Shoulder Girdle		
Chest		
Upper Back		
Lower Back		
Upper Arm		
Lower Arm		
Abdomen		
Hip / Buttock		
Upper Leg		
Lower Leg		

Notes

Today I Experienced			
Headache / Migraine		Diarrhoea	
Muscle Twinges / Cramps		Constipation	
Muscle Weakness		Bloating / Stomach Pain / IBS	
Skin Itching / Burning / Hives / Rash (circle all that apply)		Bladder Issues	
Bruising		Swelling	
Sweating		Stress	
Nervousness		Nausea / vomiting	
Sensitive to Sensory Stimulation (light / noise / temperature)		Numbness / Tingling (name part of body)	
Dizziness		Missed meal / unusual food	
Loss of appetite		Hormonal Changes	
Other:		Other:	
Other:		Other:	

Date: ***Weather:***

Hours Slept: Insomnia? Yes ☐ No ☐

How did you feel on waking today? I felt refreshed: ☐

Slightly unrefreshed: ☐ Moderately unrefreshed: ☐ Severely unrefreshed: ☐

Did you exercise today? Yes ☐ No ☐

		Morning	Afternoon	Evening
	3			
	2			
	1			
Fatigue	0			
	3			
	2			
	1			
Pain Levels	0			
	3			
	2			
	1			
Cognitive Symptoms / Brain Fog	0			

		Morning	Afternoon	Evening
	3			
	2			
	1			
Anxiety / Low Mood	0			
	3			
	2			
	1			
Activity Levels	0			
	3			
	2			
	1			
Other	0			

Symptom Score: 0 = No problem, 1 = Slight, 2 = Moderate, 3 = Severe. See p.3

Today's Notes:

Pain Location & Levels

Shade bodies, tick boxes or use pain score.

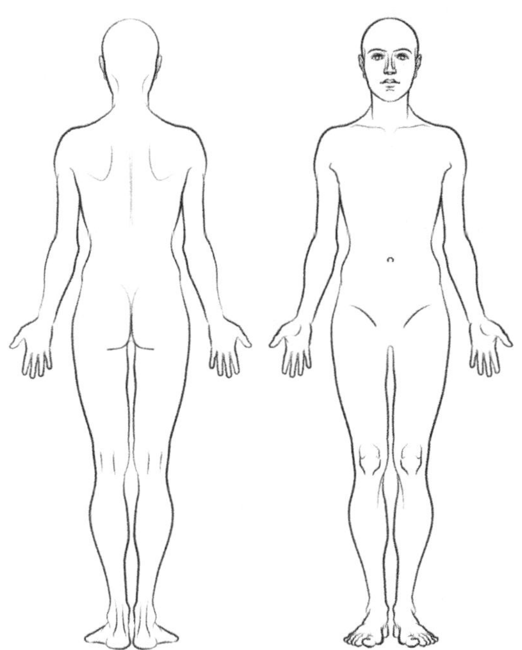

Pain Score
1 = Slight, 2 = Moderate, 3 = Severe.

	Left	Right
Jaw		
Neck		
Shoulder Girdle		
Chest		
Upper Back		
Lower Back		
Upper Arm		
Lower Arm		
Abdomen		
Hip / Buttock		
Upper Leg		
Lower Leg		

Notes

Today I Experienced			
Headache / Migraine		Diarrhoea	
Muscle Twinges / Cramps		Constipation	
Muscle Weakness		Bloating / Stomach Pain / IBS	
Skin Itching / Burning / Hives / Rash (circle all that apply)		Bladder Issues	
Bruising		Swelling	
Sweating		Stress	
Nervousness		Nausea / vomiting	
Sensitive to Sensory Stimulation (light / noise / temperature)		Numbness / Tingling (name part of body)	
Dizziness		Missed meal / unusual food	
Loss of appetite		Hormonal Changes	
Other:		Other:	
Other:		Other:	

Date: ***Weather:***

Hours Slept: Insomnia? Yes ☐ No ☐

How did you feel on waking today? I felt refreshed: ☐

Slightly unrefreshed: ☐ Moderately unrefreshed: ☐ Severely unrefreshed: ☐

Did you exercise today? Yes ☐ No ☐

		Morning	Afternoon	Evening
Fatigue	3			
	2			
	1			
	0			
Pain Levels	3			
	2			
	1			
	0			
Cognitive Symptoms / Brain Fog	3			
	2			
	1			
	0			

		Morning	Afternoon	Evening
Anxiety / Low Mood	3			
	2			
	1			
	0			
Activity Levels	3			
	2			
	1			
	0			
Other	3			
	2			
	1			
	0			

Symptom Score: 0 = No problem, 1 = Slight, 2 = Moderate, 3 = Severe. See p.3

Today's Notes:

Pain Location & Levels

Shade bodies, tick boxes or use pain score.

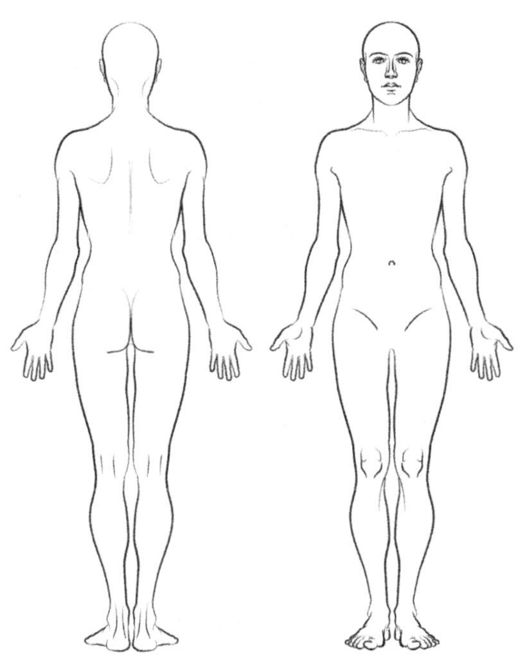

Pain Score
1 = Slight, 2 = Moderate, 3 = Severe.

	Left	Right
Jaw		
Neck		
Shoulder Girdle		
Chest		
Upper Back		
Lower Back		
Upper Arm		
Lower Arm		
Abdomen		
Hip / Buttock		
Upper Leg		
Lower Leg		

Notes

Today I Experienced			
Headache / Migraine		Diarrhoea	
Muscle Twinges / Cramps		Constipation	
Muscle Weakness		Bloating / Stomach Pain / IBS	
Skin Itching / Burning / Hives / Rash (circle all that apply)		Bladder Issues	
Bruising		Swelling	
Sweating		Stress	
Nervousness		Nausea / vomiting	
Sensitive to Sensory Stimulation (light / noise / temperature)		Numbness / Tingling (name part of body)	
Dizziness		Missed meal / unusual food	
Loss of appetite		Hormonal Changes	
Other:		Other:	
Other:		Other:	

Date: ***Weather:***

Hours Slept: Insomnia? Yes ☐ No ☐

How did you feel on waking today? I felt refreshed: ☐

Slightly unrefreshed: ☐ Moderately unrefreshed: ☐ Severely unrefreshed: ☐

Did you exercise today? Yes ☐ No ☐

		Morning	Afternoon	Evening
Fatigue	3			
	2			
	1			
	0			
Pain Levels	3			
	2			
	1			
	0			
Cognitive Symptoms / Brain Fog	3			
	2			
	1			
	0			

		Morning	Afternoon	Evening
Anxiety / Low Mood	3			
	2			
	1			
	0			
Activity Levels	3			
	2			
	1			
	0			
Other	3			
	2			
	1			
	0			

Symptom Score: 0 = No problem, 1 = Slight, 2 = Moderate, 3 = Severe. See p.3

Today's Notes:

Pain Location & Levels

Shade bodies, tick boxes or use pain score.

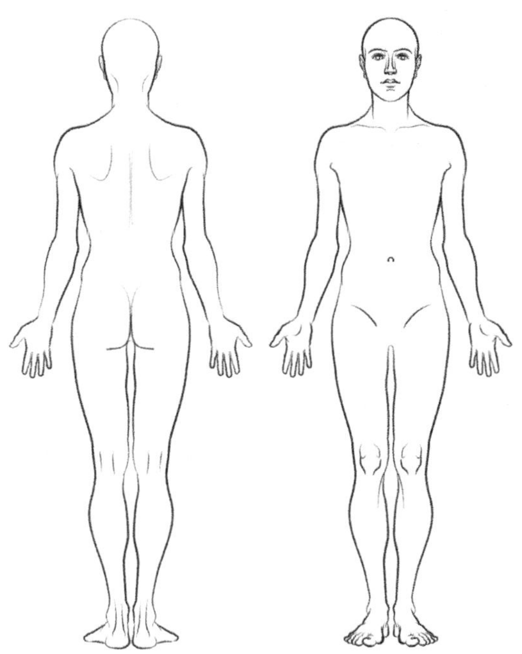

Pain Score
1 = Slight, 2 = Moderate, 3 = Severe.

	Left	Right
Jaw		
Neck		
Shoulder Girdle		
Chest		
Upper Back		
Lower Back		
Upper Arm		
Lower Arm		
Abdomen		
Hip / Buttock		
Upper Leg		
Lower Leg		

Notes

Today I Experienced			
Headache / Migraine		Diarrhoea	
Muscle Twinges / Cramps		Constipation	
Muscle Weakness		Bloating / Stomach Pain / IBS	
Skin Itching / Burning / Hives / Rash (circle all that apply)		Bladder Issues	
Bruising		Swelling	
Sweating		Stress	
Nervousness		Nausea / vomiting	
Sensitive to Sensory Stimulation (light / noise / temperature)		Numbness / Tingling (name part of body)	
Dizziness		Missed meal / unusual food	
Loss of appetite		Hormonal Changes	
Other:		Other:	
Other:		Other:	

Date: ***Weather:***

Hours Slept: Insomnia? Yes ☐ No ☐

How did you feel on waking today? I felt refreshed: ☐

Slightly unrefreshed: ☐ Moderately unrefreshed: ☐ Severely unrefreshed: ☐

Did you exercise today? Yes ☐ No ☐

		Morning	Afternoon	Evening
Fatigue	3			
	2			
	1			
	0			
Pain Levels	3			
	2			
	1			
	0			
Cognitive Symptoms / Brain Fog	3			
	2			
	1			
	0			

		Morning	Afternoon	Evening
Anxiety / Low Mood	3			
	2			
	1			
	0			
Activity Levels	3			
	2			
	1			
	0			
Other	3			
	2			
	1			
	0			

Symptom Score: 0 = No problem, 1 = Slight, 2 = Moderate, 3 = Severe. See p.3

Today's Notes:

Pain Location & Levels

Shade bodies, tick boxes or use pain score.

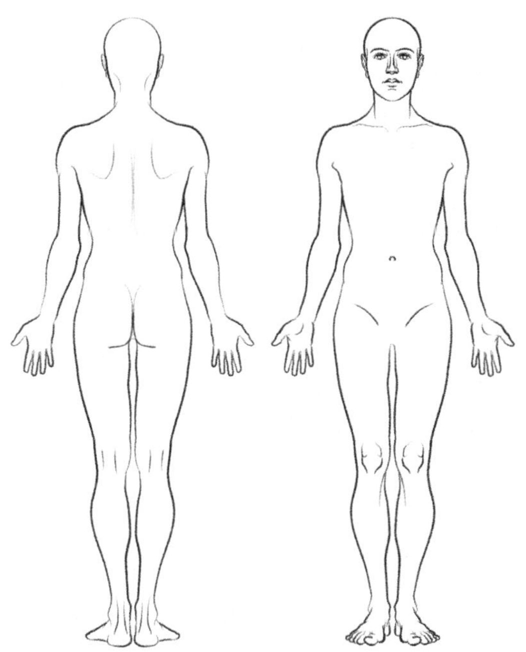

Pain Score
1 = Slight, 2 = Moderate, 3 = Severe.

	Left	Right
Jaw		
Neck		
Shoulder Girdle		
Chest		
Upper Back		
Lower Back		
Upper Arm		
Lower Arm		
Abdomen		
Hip / Buttock		
Upper Leg		
Lower Leg		

Notes

Today I Experienced			
Headache / Migraine		Diarrhoea	
Muscle Twinges / Cramps		Constipation	
Muscle Weakness		Bloating / Stomach Pain / IBS	
Skin Itching / Burning / Hives / Rash (circle all that apply)		Bladder Issues	
Bruising		Swelling	
Sweating		Stress	
Nervousness		Nausea / vomiting	
Sensitive to Sensory Stimulation (light / noise / temperature)		Numbness / Tingling (name part of body)	
Dizziness		Missed meal / unusual food	
Loss of appetite		Hormonal Changes	
Other:		Other:	
Other:		Other:	

Date: ***Weather:***

Hours Slept: Insomnia? Yes ☐ No ☐

How did you feel on waking today? I felt refreshed: ☐

Slightly unrefreshed: ☐ Moderately unrefreshed: ☐ Severely unrefreshed: ☐

Did you exercise today? Yes ☐ No ☐

		Morning	Afternoon	Evening
Fatigue	3			
	2			
	1			
	0			
Pain Levels	3			
	2			
	1			
	0			
Cognitive Symptoms / Brain Fog	3			
	2			
	1			
	0			

		Morning	Afternoon	Evening
Anxiety / Low Mood	3			
	2			
	1			
	0			
Activity Levels	3			
	2			
	1			
	0			
Other	3			
	2			
	1			
	0			

Symptom Score: 0 = No problem, 1 = Slight, 2 = Moderate, 3 = Severe. See p.3

Today's Notes:

Pain Location & Levels

Shade bodies, tick boxes or use pain score.

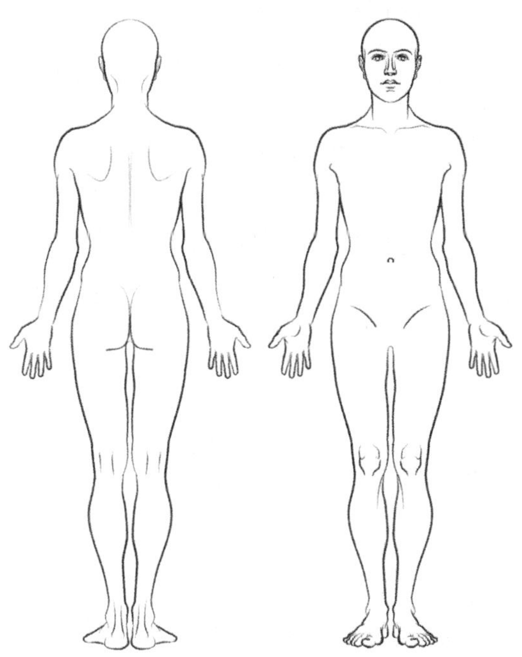

Pain Score
1 = Slight, 2 = Moderate, 3 = Severe.

	Left	Right
Jaw		
Neck		
Shoulder Girdle		
Chest		
Upper Back		
Lower Back		
Upper Arm		
Lower Arm		
Abdomen		
Hip / Buttock		
Upper Leg		
Lower Leg		

Notes

Today I Experienced			
Headache / Migraine		Diarrhoea	
Muscle Twinges / Cramps		Constipation	
Muscle Weakness		Bloating / Stomach Pain / IBS	
Skin Itching / Burning / Hives / Rash (circle all that apply)		Bladder Issues	
Bruising		Swelling	
Sweating		Stress	
Nervousness		Nausea / vomiting	
Sensitive to Sensory Stimulation (light / noise / temperature)		Numbness / Tingling (name part of body)	
Dizziness		Missed meal / unusual food	
Loss of appetite		Hormonal Changes	
Other:		Other:	
Other:		Other:	

Date: ***Weather:***

Hours Slept: Insomnia? Yes ☐ No ☐

How did you feel on waking today? I felt refreshed: ☐

Slightly unrefreshed: ☐ Moderately unrefreshed: ☐ Severely unrefreshed: ☐

Did you exercise today? Yes ☐ No ☐

		Morning	Afternoon	Evening
Fatigue	3			
	2			
	1			
	0			
Pain Levels	3			
	2			
	1			
	0			
Cognitive Symptoms / Brain Fog	3			
	2			
	1			
	0			

		Morning	Afternoon	Evening
Anxiety / Low Mood	3			
	2			
	1			
	0			
Activity Levels	3			
	2			
	1			
	0			
Other	3			
	2			
	1			
	0			

Symptom Score: 0 = No problem, 1 = Slight, 2 = Moderate, 3 = Severe. See p.3

Today's Notes:

Pain Location & Levels

Shade bodies, tick boxes or use pain score.

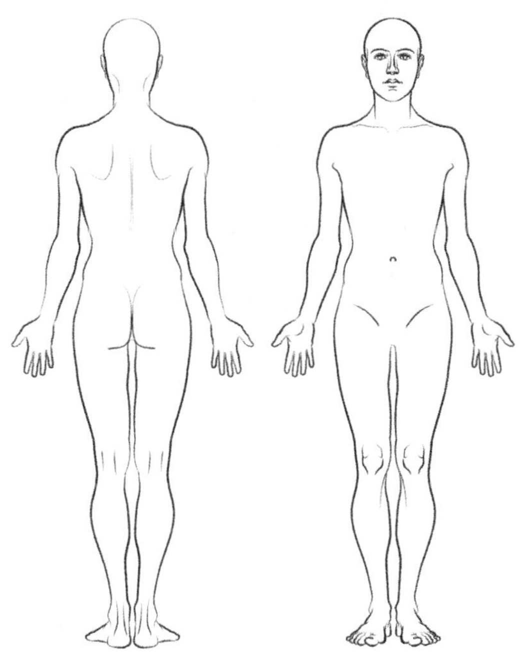

Pain Score
1 = Slight, 2 = Moderate, 3 = Severe.

	Left	Right
Jaw		
Neck		
Shoulder Girdle		
Chest		
Upper Back		
Lower Back		
Upper Arm		
Lower Arm		
Abdomen		
Hip / Buttock		
Upper Leg		
Lower Leg		

Notes

Today I Experienced			
Headache / Migraine		Diarrhoea	
Muscle Twinges / Cramps		Constipation	
Muscle Weakness		Bloating / Stomach Pain / IBS	
Skin Itching / Burning / Hives / Rash (circle all that apply)		Bladder Issues	
Bruising		Swelling	
Sweating		Stress	
Nervousness		Nausea / vomiting	
Sensitive to Sensory Stimulation (light / noise / temperature)		Numbness / Tingling (name part of body)	
Dizziness		Missed meal / unusual food	
Loss of appetite		Hormonal Changes	
Other:		Other:	
Other:		Other:	

Date: ***Weather:***

Hours Slept: Insomnia? Yes ☐ No ☐

How did you feel on waking today? I felt refreshed: ☐

Slightly unrefreshed: ☐ Moderately unrefreshed: ☐ Severely unrefreshed: ☐

Did you exercise today? Yes ☐ No ☐

		Morning	Afternoon	Evening
Fatigue	3			
	2			
	1			
	0			
Pain Levels	3			
	2			
	1			
	0			
Cognitive Symptoms / Brain Fog	3			
	2			
	1			
	0			

		Morning	Afternoon	Evening
Anxiety / Low Mood	3			
	2			
	1			
	0			
Activity Levels	3			
	2			
	1			
	0			
Other	3			
	2			
	1			
	0			

Symptom Score: 0 = No problem, 1 = Slight, 2 = Moderate, 3 = Severe. See p.3

Today's Notes:

Pain Location & Levels

Shade bodies, tick boxes or use pain score.

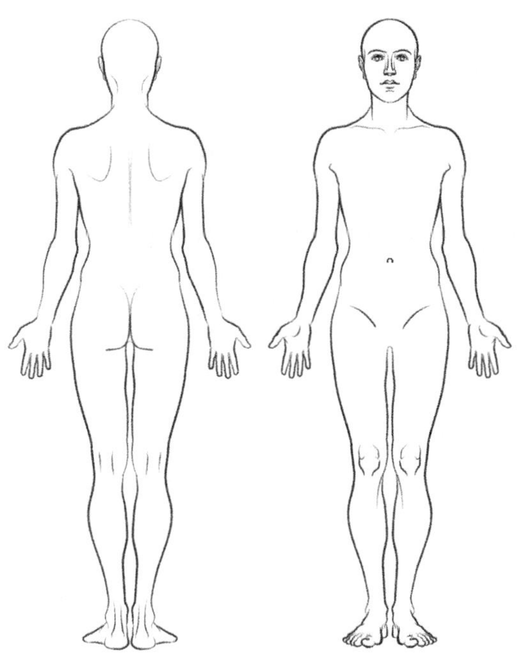

Pain Score
1 = Slight, 2 = Moderate, 3 = Severe.

	Left	Right
Jaw		
Neck		
Shoulder Girdle		
Chest		
Upper Back		
Lower Back		
Upper Arm		
Lower Arm		
Abdomen		
Hip / Buttock		
Upper Leg		
Lower Leg		

Notes

Today I Experienced			
Headache / Migraine		Diarrhoea	
Muscle Twinges / Cramps		Constipation	
Muscle Weakness		Bloating / Stomach Pain / IBS	
Skin Itching / Burning / Hives / Rash (circle all that apply)		Bladder Issues	
Bruising		Swelling	
Sweating		Stress	
Nervousness		Nausea / vomiting	
Sensitive to Sensory Stimulation (light / noise / temperature)		Numbness / Tingling (name part of body)	
Dizziness		Missed meal / unusual food	
Loss of appetite		Hormonal Changes	
Other:		Other:	
Other:		Other:	

Date: ***Weather:***

Hours Slept: Insomnia? Yes ☐ No ☐

How did you feel on waking today? I felt refreshed: ☐

Slightly unrefreshed: ☐ Moderately unrefreshed: ☐ Severely unrefreshed: ☐

Did you exercise today? Yes ☐ No ☐

		Morning	Afternoon	Evening
Fatigue	3			
	2			
	1			
	0			
Pain Levels	3			
	2			
	1			
	0			
Cognitive Symptoms / Brain Fog	3			
	2			
	1			
	0			

		Morning	Afternoon	Evening
Anxiety / Low Mood	3			
	2			
	1			
	0			
Activity Levels	3			
	2			
	1			
	0			
Other	3			
	2			
	1			
	0			

Symptom Score: 0 = No problem, 1 = Slight, 2 = Moderate, 3 = Severe. See p.3

Today's Notes:

Pain Location & Levels

Shade bodies, tick boxes or use pain score.

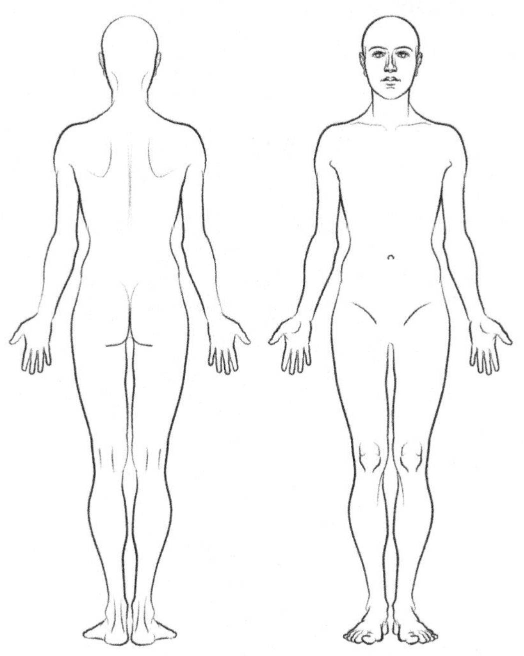

Pain Score
1 = Slight, 2 = Moderate, 3 = Severe.

	Left	Right
Jaw		
Neck		
Shoulder Girdle		
Chest		
Upper Back		
Lower Back		
Upper Arm		
Lower Arm		
Abdomen		
Hip / Buttock		
Upper Leg		
Lower Leg		

Notes

Today I Experienced			
Headache / Migraine		Diarrhoea	
Muscle Twinges / Cramps		Constipation	
Muscle Weakness		Bloating / Stomach Pain / IBS	
Skin Itching / Burning / Hives / Rash (circle all that apply)		Bladder Issues	
Bruising		Swelling	
Sweating		Stress	
Nervousness		Nausea / vomiting	
Sensitive to Sensory Stimulation (light / noise / temperature)		Numbness / Tingling (name part of body)	
Dizziness		Missed meal / unusual food	
Loss of appetite		Hormonal Changes	
Other:		Other:	
Other:		Other:	

Date: ***Weather:***

Hours Slept: Insomnia? Yes ☐ No ☐

How did you feel on waking today? I felt refreshed: ☐

Slightly unrefreshed: ☐ Moderately unrefreshed: ☐ Severely unrefreshed: ☐

Did you exercise today? Yes ☐ No ☐

		Morning	Afternoon	Evening
Fatigue	3			
	2			
	1			
	0			
Pain Levels	3			
	2			
	1			
	0			
Cognitive Symptoms / Brain Fog	3			
	2			
	1			
	0			

		Morning	Afternoon	Evening
Anxiety / Low Mood	3			
	2			
	1			
	0			
Activity Levels	3			
	2			
	1			
	0			
Other	3			
	2			
	1			
	0			

Symptom Score: 0 = No problem, 1 = Slight, 2 = Moderate, 3 = Severe. See p.3

Today's Notes:

Pain Location & Levels

Shade bodies, tick boxes or use pain score.

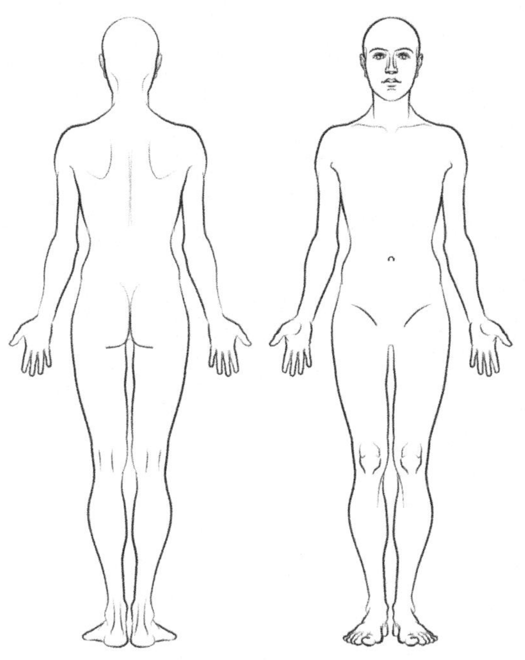

Pain Score
1 = Slight, 2 = Moderate, 3 = Severe.

	Left	Right
Jaw		
Neck		
Shoulder Girdle		
Chest		
Upper Back		
Lower Back		
Upper Arm		
Lower Arm		
Abdomen		
Hip / Buttock		
Upper Leg		
Lower Leg		

Notes

Today I Experienced			
Headache / Migraine		Diarrhoea	
Muscle Twinges / Cramps		Constipation	
Muscle Weakness		Bloating / Stomach Pain / IBS	
Skin Itching / Burning / Hives / Rash (circle all that apply)		Bladder Issues	
Bruising		Swelling	
Sweating		Stress	
Nervousness		Nausea / vomiting	
Sensitive to Sensory Stimulation (light / noise / temperature)		Numbness / Tingling (name part of body)	
Dizziness		Missed meal / unusual food	
Loss of appetite		Hormonal Changes	
Other:		Other:	
Other:		Other:	

Date: ***Weather:***

Hours Slept: Insomnia? Yes ☐ No ☐

How did you feel on waking today? I felt refreshed: ☐

Slightly unrefreshed: ☐ Moderately unrefreshed: ☐ Severely unrefreshed: ☐

Did you exercise today? Yes ☐ No ☐

		Morning	Afternoon	Evening
Fatigue	3			
	2			
	1			
	0			
Pain Levels	3			
	2			
	1			
	0			
Cognitive Symptoms / Brain Fog	3			
	2			
	1			
	0			

		Morning	Afternoon	Evening
Anxiety / Low Mood	3			
	2			
	1			
	0			
Activity Levels	3			
	2			
	1			
	0			
Other	3			
	2			
	1			
	0			

Symptom Score: 0 = No problem, 1 = Slight, 2 = Moderate, 3 = Severe. See p.3

Today's Notes:

Pain Location & Levels

Shade bodies, tick boxes or use pain score.

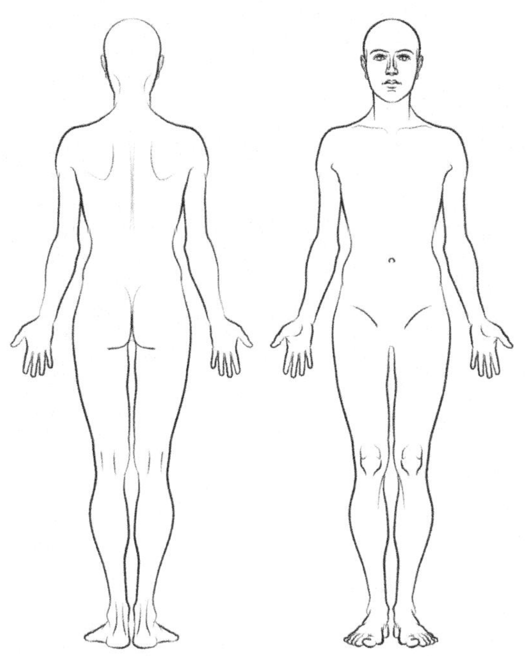

Pain Score
1 = Slight, 2 = Moderate, 3 = Severe.

	Left	Right
Jaw		
Neck		
Shoulder Girdle		
Chest		
Upper Back		
Lower Back		
Upper Arm		
Lower Arm		
Abdomen		
Hip / Buttock		
Upper Leg		
Lower Leg		

Notes

Today I Experienced			
Headache / Migraine		Diarrhoea	
Muscle Twinges / Cramps		Constipation	
Muscle Weakness		Bloating / Stomach Pain / IBS	
Skin Itching / Burning / Hives / Rash (circle all that apply)		Bladder Issues	
Bruising		Swelling	
Sweating		Stress	
Nervousness		Nausea / vomiting	
Sensitive to Sensory Stimulation (light / noise / temperature)		Numbness / Tingling (name part of body)	
Dizziness		Missed meal / unusual food	
Loss of appetite		Hormonal Changes	
Other:		Other:	
Other:		Other:	

Date: ***Weather:***

Hours Slept: Insomnia? Yes ☐ No ☐

How did you feel on waking today? I felt refreshed: ☐

Slightly unrefreshed: ☐ Moderately unrefreshed: ☐ Severely unrefreshed: ☐

Did you exercise today? Yes ☐ No ☐

		Morning	Afternoon	Evening
Fatigue	3			
	2			
	1			
	0			
Pain Levels	3			
	2			
	1			
	0			
Cognitive Symptoms / Brain Fog	3			
	2			
	1			
	0			

		Morning	Afternoon	Evening
Anxiety / Low Mood	3			
	2			
	1			
	0			
Activity Levels	3			
	2			
	1			
	0			
Other	3			
	2			
	1			
	0			

Symptom Score: 0 = No problem, 1 = Slight, 2 = Moderate, 3 = Severe. See p.3

Today's Notes:

Pain Location & Levels

Shade bodies, tick boxes or use pain score.

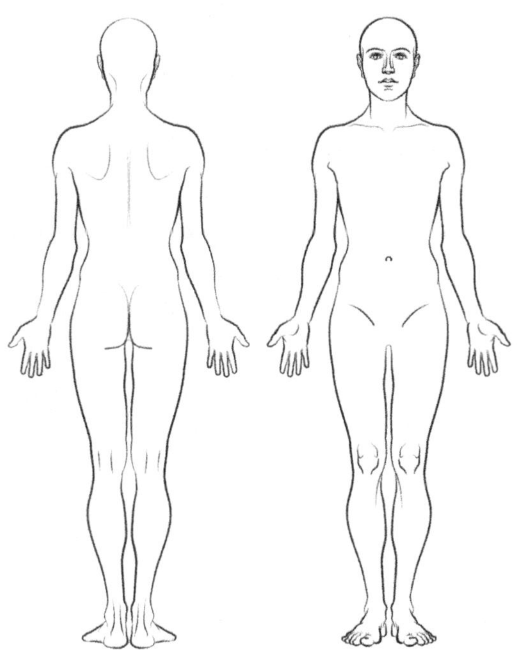

Pain Score
1 = Slight, 2 = Moderate, 3 = Severe.

	Left	Right
Jaw		
Neck		
Shoulder Girdle		
Chest		
Upper Back		
Lower Back		
Upper Arm		
Lower Arm		
Abdomen		
Hip / Buttock		
Upper Leg		
Lower Leg		

Notes

Today I Experienced			
Headache / Migraine		Diarrhoea	
Muscle Twinges / Cramps		Constipation	
Muscle Weakness		Bloating / Stomach Pain / IBS	
Skin Itching / Burning / Hives / Rash (circle all that apply)		Bladder Issues	
Bruising		Swelling	
Sweating		Stress	
Nervousness		Nausea / vomiting	
Sensitive to Sensory Stimulation (light / noise / temperature)		Numbness / Tingling (name part of body)	
Dizziness		Missed meal / unusual food	
Loss of appetite		Hormonal Changes	
Other:		Other:	
Other:		Other:	

Date: ***Weather:***

Hours Slept: Insomnia? Yes ☐ No ☐

How did you feel on waking today? I felt refreshed: ☐

Slightly unrefreshed: ☐ Moderately unrefreshed: ☐ Severely unrefreshed: ☐

Did you exercise today? Yes ☐ No ☐

		Morning	Afternoon	Evening
	3			
	2			
	1			
Fatigue	0			
	3			
	2			
	1			
Pain Levels	0			
	3			
	2			
	1			
Cognitive Symptoms / Brain Fog	0			

		Morning	Afternoon	Evening
	3			
	2			
	1			
Anxiety / Low Mood	0			
	3			
	2			
	1			
Activity Levels	0			
	3			
	2			
	1			
Other	0			

Symptom Score: 0 = No problem, 1 = Slight, 2 = Moderate, 3 = Severe. See p.3

Today's Notes:

Pain Location & Levels

Shade bodies, tick boxes or use pain score.

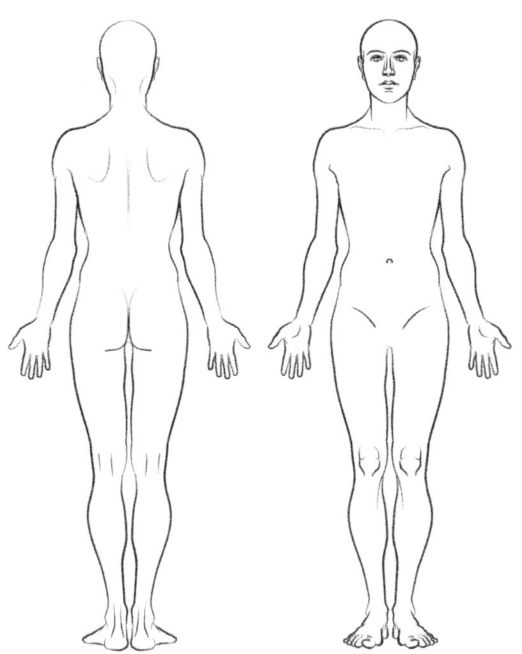

Pain Score
1 = Slight, 2 = Moderate, 3 = Severe.

	Left	Right
Jaw		
Neck		
Shoulder Girdle		
Chest		
Upper Back		
Lower Back		
Upper Arm		
Lower Arm		
Abdomen		
Hip / Buttock		
Upper Leg		
Lower Leg		

Notes

Today I Experienced			
Headache / Migraine		Diarrhoea	
Muscle Twinges / Cramps		Constipation	
Muscle Weakness		Bloating / Stomach Pain / IBS	
Skin Itching / Burning / Hives / Rash (circle all that apply)		Bladder Issues	
Bruising		Swelling	
Sweating		Stress	
Nervousness		Nausea / vomiting	
Sensitive to Sensory Stimulation (light / noise / temperature)		Numbness / Tingling (name part of body)	
Dizziness		Missed meal / unusual food	
Loss of appetite		Hormonal Changes	
Other:		Other:	
Other:		Other:	

Date: ***Weather:***

Hours Slept: Insomnia? Yes ☐ No ☐

How did you feel on waking today? I felt refreshed: ☐

Slightly unrefreshed: ☐ Moderately unrefreshed: ☐ Severely unrefreshed: ☐

Did you exercise today? Yes ☐ No ☐

		Morning	Afternoon	Evening
Fatigue	3			
	2			
	1			
	0			
Pain Levels	3			
	2			
	1			
	0			
Cognitive Symptoms / Brain Fog	3			
	2			
	1			
	0			

		Morning	Afternoon	Evening
Anxiety / Low Mood	3			
	2			
	1			
	0			
Activity Levels	3			
	2			
	1			
	0			
Other	3			
	2			
	1			
	0			

Symptom Score: 0 = No problem, 1 = Slight, 2 = Moderate, 3 = Severe. See p.3

Today's Notes:

Pain Location & Levels

Shade bodies, tick boxes or use pain score.

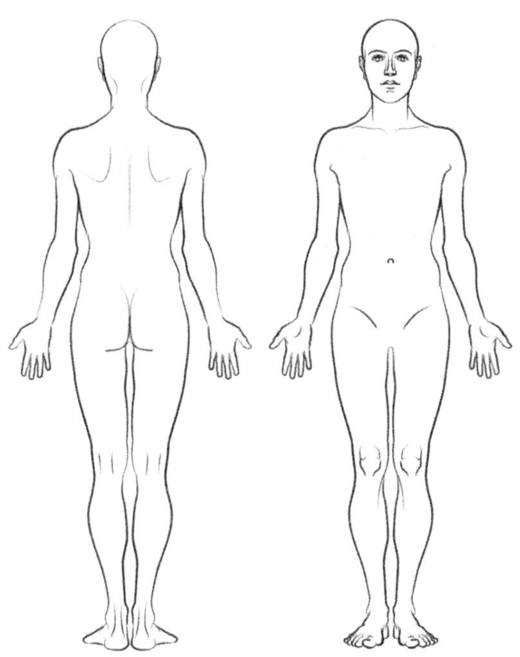

Pain Score
1 = Slight, 2 = Moderate, 3 = Severe.

	Left	Right
Jaw		
Neck		
Shoulder Girdle		
Chest		
Upper Back		
Lower Back		
Upper Arm		
Lower Arm		
Abdomen		
Hip / Buttock		
Upper Leg		
Lower Leg		

Notes

Today I Experienced			
Headache / Migraine		Diarrhoea	
Muscle Twinges / Cramps		Constipation	
Muscle Weakness		Bloating / Stomach Pain / IBS	
Skin Itching / Burning / Hives / Rash (circle all that apply)		Bladder Issues	
Bruising		Swelling	
Sweating		Stress	
Nervousness		Nausea / vomiting	
Sensitive to Sensory Stimulation (light / noise / temperature)		Numbness / Tingling (name part of body)	
Dizziness		Missed meal / unusual food	
Loss of appetite		Hormonal Changes	
Other:		Other:	
Other:		Other:	

Date: ***Weather:***

Hours Slept: Insomnia? Yes ☐ No ☐

How did you feel on waking today? I felt refreshed: ☐

Slightly unrefreshed: ☐ Moderately unrefreshed: ☐ Severely unrefreshed: ☐

Did you exercise today? Yes ☐ No ☐

		Morning	Afternoon	Evening
Fatigue	3			
	2			
	1			
	0			
Pain Levels	3			
	2			
	1			
	0			
Cognitive Symptoms / Brain Fog	3			
	2			
	1			
	0			

		Morning	Afternoon	Evening
Anxiety / Low Mood	3			
	2			
	1			
	0			
Activity Levels	3			
	2			
	1			
	0			
Other	3			
	2			
	1			
	0			

Symptom Score: 0 = No problem, 1 = Slight, 2 = Moderate, 3 = Severe. See p.3

Today's Notes:

Pain Location & Levels

Shade bodies, tick boxes or use pain score.

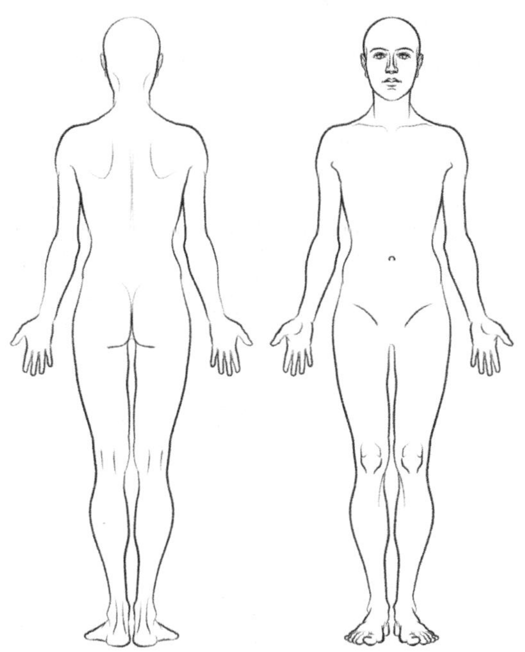

Pain Score
1 = Slight, 2 = Moderate, 3 = Severe.

	Left	Right
Jaw		
Neck		
Shoulder Girdle		
Chest		
Upper Back		
Lower Back		
Upper Arm		
Lower Arm		
Abdomen		
Hip / Buttock		
Upper Leg		
Lower Leg		

Notes

Today I Experienced			
Headache / Migraine		Diarrhoea	
Muscle Twinges / Cramps		Constipation	
Muscle Weakness		Bloating / Stomach Pain / IBS	
Skin Itching / Burning / Hives / Rash (circle all that apply)		Bladder Issues	
Bruising		Swelling	
Sweating		Stress	
Nervousness		Nausea / vomiting	
Sensitive to Sensory Stimulation (light / noise / temperature)		Numbness / Tingling (name part of body)	
Dizziness		Missed meal / unusual food	
Loss of appetite		Hormonal Changes	
Other:		Other:	
Other:		Other:	

Date: ***Weather:***

Hours Slept: Insomnia? Yes ☐ No ☐

How did you feel on waking today? I felt refreshed: ☐

Slightly unrefreshed: ☐ Moderately unrefreshed: ☐ Severely unrefreshed: ☐

Did you exercise today? Yes ☐ No ☐

		Morning	Afternoon	Evening
Fatigue	3			
	2			
	1			
	0			
Pain Levels	3			
	2			
	1			
	0			
Cognitive Symptoms / Brain Fog	3			
	2			
	1			
	0			

		Morning	Afternoon	Evening
Anxiety / Low Mood	3			
	2			
	1			
	0			
Activity Levels	3			
	2			
	1			
	0			
Other	3			
	2			
	1			
	0			

Symptom Score: 0 = No problem, 1 = Slight, 2 = Moderate, 3 = Severe. See p.3

Today's Notes:

Pain Location & Levels

Shade bodies, tick boxes or use pain score.

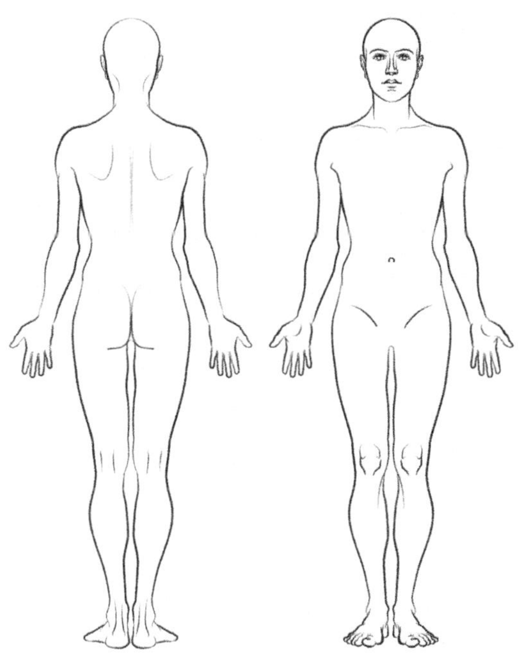

Pain Score
1 = Slight, 2 = Moderate, 3 = Severe.

	Left	Right
Jaw		
Neck		
Shoulder Girdle		
Chest		
Upper Back		
Lower Back		
Upper Arm		
Lower Arm		
Abdomen		
Hip / Buttock		
Upper Leg		
Lower Leg		

Notes

Today I Experienced			
Headache / Migraine		Diarrhoea	
Muscle Twinges / Cramps		Constipation	
Muscle Weakness		Bloating / Stomach Pain / IBS	
Skin Itching / Burning / Hives / Rash (circle all that apply)		Bladder Issues	
Bruising		Swelling	
Sweating		Stress	
Nervousness		Nausea / vomiting	
Sensitive to Sensory Stimulation (light / noise / temperature)		Numbness / Tingling (name part of body)	
Dizziness		Missed meal / unusual food	
Loss of appetite		Hormonal Changes	
Other:		Other:	
Other:		Other:	

Date: ***Weather:***

Hours Slept: Insomnia? Yes ☐ No ☐

How did you feel on waking today? I felt refreshed: ☐

Slightly unrefreshed: ☐ Moderately unrefreshed: ☐ Severely unrefreshed: ☐

Did you exercise today? Yes ☐ No ☐

		Morning	Afternoon	Evening
Fatigue	3			
	2			
	1			
	0			
Pain Levels	3			
	2			
	1			
	0			
Cognitive Symptoms / Brain Fog	3			
	2			
	1			
	0			

		Morning	Afternoon	Evening
Anxiety / Low Mood	3			
	2			
	1			
	0			
Activity Levels	3			
	2			
	1			
	0			
Other	3			
	2			
	1			
	0			

Symptom Score: 0 = No problem, 1 = Slight, 2 = Moderate, 3 = Severe. See p.3

Today's Notes:

Pain Location & Levels

Shade bodies, tick boxes or use pain score.

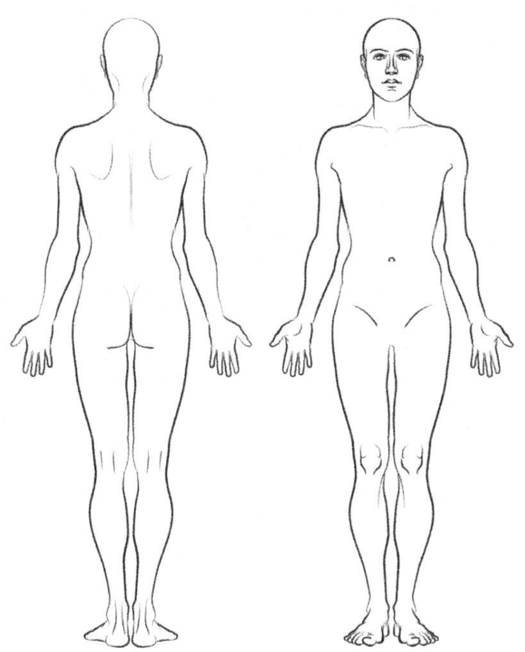

Pain Score
1 = Slight, 2 = Moderate, 3 = Severe.

	Left	Right
Jaw		
Neck		
Shoulder Girdle		
Chest		
Upper Back		
Lower Back		
Upper Arm		
Lower Arm		
Abdomen		
Hip / Buttock		
Upper Leg		
Lower Leg		

Notes

Today I Experienced			
Headache / Migraine		Diarrhoea	
Muscle Twinges / Cramps		Constipation	
Muscle Weakness		Bloating / Stomach Pain / IBS	
Skin Itching / Burning / Hives / Rash (circle all that apply)		Bladder Issues	
Bruising		Swelling	
Sweating		Stress	
Nervousness		Nausea / vomiting	
Sensitive to Sensory Stimulation (light / noise / temperature)		Numbness / Tingling (name part of body)	
Dizziness		Missed meal / unusual food	
Loss of appetite		Hormonal Changes	
Other:		Other:	
Other:		Other:	

Date: ***Weather:***

Hours Slept: Insomnia? Yes ☐ No ☐

How did you feel on waking today? I felt refreshed: ☐

Slightly unrefreshed: ☐ Moderately unrefreshed: ☐ Severely unrefreshed: ☐

Did you exercise today? Yes ☐ No ☐

		Morning	Afternoon	Evening
Fatigue	3			
	2			
	1			
	0			
Pain Levels	3			
	2			
	1			
	0			
Cognitive Symptoms / Brain Fog	3			
	2			
	1			
	0			

		Morning	Afternoon	Evening
Anxiety / Low Mood	3			
	2			
	1			
	0			
Activity Levels	3			
	2			
	1			
	0			
Other	3			
	2			
	1			
	0			

Symptom Score: 0 = No problem, 1 = Slight, 2 = Moderate, 3 = Severe. See p.3

Today's Notes:

Pain Location & Levels

Shade bodies, tick boxes or use pain score.

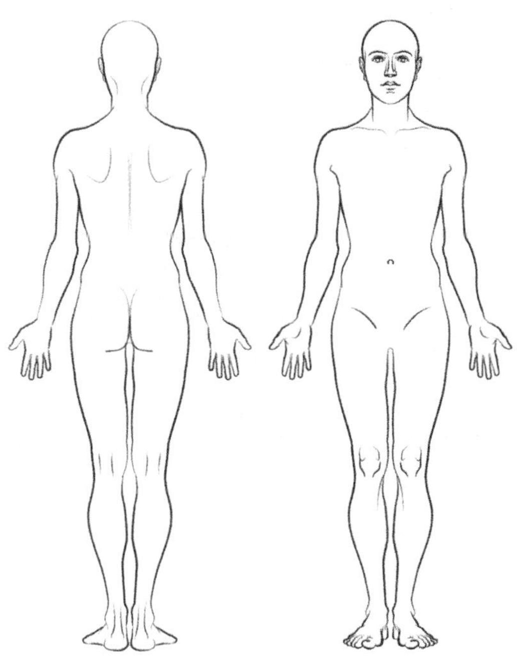

Pain Score
1 = Slight, 2 = Moderate, 3 = Severe.

	Left	Right
Jaw		
Neck		
Shoulder Girdle		
Chest		
Upper Back		
Lower Back		
Upper Arm		
Lower Arm		
Abdomen		
Hip / Buttock		
Upper Leg		
Lower Leg		

Notes

Today I Experienced			
Headache / Migraine		Diarrhoea	
Muscle Twinges / Cramps		Constipation	
Muscle Weakness		Bloating / Stomach Pain / IBS	
Skin Itching / Burning / Hives / Rash (circle all that apply)		Bladder Issues	
Bruising		Swelling	
Sweating		Stress	
Nervousness		Nausea / vomiting	
Sensitive to Sensory Stimulation (light / noise / temperature)		Numbness / Tingling (name part of body)	
Dizziness		Missed meal / unusual food	
Loss of appetite		Hormonal Changes	
Other:		Other:	
Other:		Other:	

Date: ***Weather:***

Hours Slept: Insomnia? Yes ☐ No ☐

How did you feel on waking today? I felt refreshed: ☐

Slightly unrefreshed: ☐ Moderately unrefreshed: ☐ Severely unrefreshed: ☐

Did you exercise today? Yes ☐ No ☐

		Morning	Afternoon	Evening
	3			
	2			
	1			
Fatigue	0			
	3			
	2			
	1			
Pain Levels	0			
	3			
	2			
	1			
Cognitive Symptoms / Brain Fog	0			

		Morning	Afternoon	Evening
	3			
	2			
	1			
Anxiety / Low Mood	0			
	3			
	2			
	1			
Activity Levels	0			
	3			
	2			
	1			
Other	0			

Symptom Score: 0 = No problem, 1 = Slight, 2 = Moderate, 3 = Severe. See p.3

Today's Notes:

Pain Location & Levels

Shade bodies, tick boxes or use pain score.

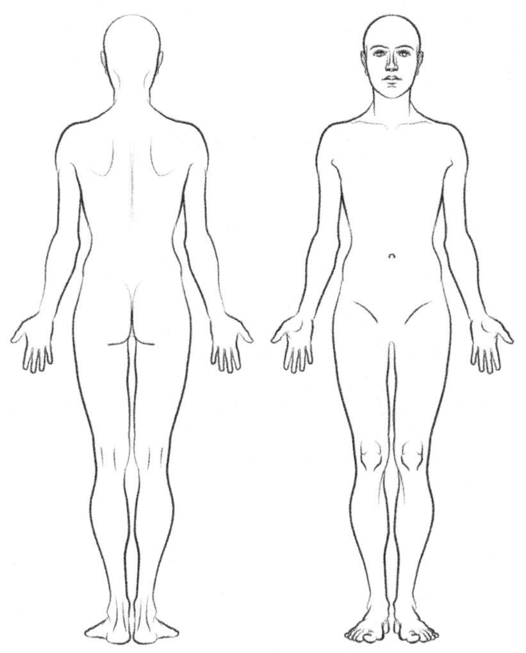

Pain Score
1 = Slight, 2 = Moderate, 3 = Severe.

	Left	Right
Jaw		
Neck		
Shoulder Girdle		
Chest		
Upper Back		
Lower Back		
Upper Arm		
Lower Arm		
Abdomen		
Hip / Buttock		
Upper Leg		
Lower Leg		

Notes

Today I Experienced			
Headache / Migraine		Diarrhoea	
Muscle Twinges / Cramps		Constipation	
Muscle Weakness		Bloating / Stomach Pain / IBS	
Skin Itching / Burning / Hives / Rash (circle all that apply)		Bladder Issues	
Bruising		Swelling	
Sweating		Stress	
Nervousness		Nausea / vomiting	
Sensitive to Sensory Stimulation (light / noise / temperature)		Numbness / Tingling (name part of body)	
Dizziness		Missed meal / unusual food	
Loss of appetite		Hormonal Changes	
Other:		Other:	
Other:		Other:	

Date: ***Weather:***

Hours Slept: Insomnia? Yes ☐ No ☐

How did you feel on waking today? I felt refreshed: ☐

Slightly unrefreshed: ☐ Moderately unrefreshed: ☐ Severely unrefreshed: ☐

Did you exercise today? Yes ☐ No ☐

		Morning	Afternoon	Evening
Fatigue	3			
	2			
	1			
	0			
Pain Levels	3			
	2			
	1			
	0			
Cognitive Symptoms / Brain Fog	3			
	2			
	1			
	0			

		Morning	Afternoon	Evening
Anxiety / Low Mood	3			
	2			
	1			
	0			
Activity Levels	3			
	2			
	1			
	0			
Other	3			
	2			
	1			
	0			

Symptom Score: 0 = No problem, 1 = Slight, 2 = Moderate, 3 = Severe. See p.3

Today's Notes:

Pain Location & Levels

Shade bodies, tick boxes or use pain score.

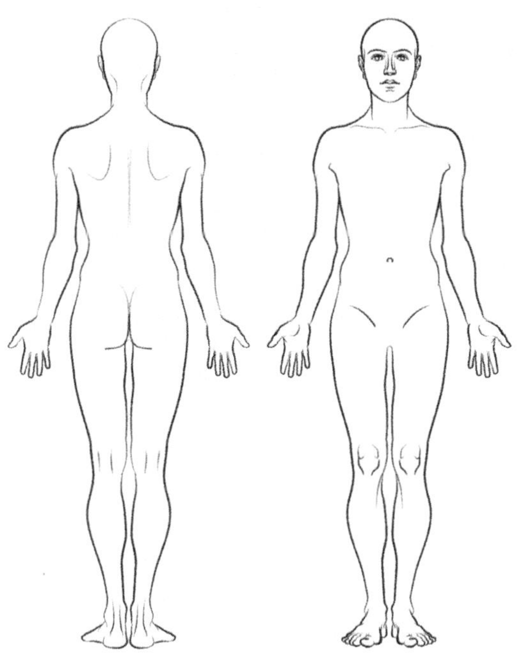

Pain Score
1 = Slight, 2 = Moderate, 3 = Severe.

	Left	Right
Jaw		
Neck		
Shoulder Girdle		
Chest		
Upper Back		
Lower Back		
Upper Arm		
Lower Arm		
Abdomen		
Hip / Buttock		
Upper Leg		
Lower Leg		

Notes

Today I Experienced			
Headache / Migraine		Diarrhoea	
Muscle Twinges / Cramps		Constipation	
Muscle Weakness		Bloating / Stomach Pain / IBS	
Skin Itching / Burning / Hives / Rash (circle all that apply)		Bladder Issues	
Bruising		Swelling	
Sweating		Stress	
Nervousness		Nausea / vomiting	
Sensitive to Sensory Stimulation (light / noise / temperature)		Numbness / Tingling (name part of body)	
Dizziness		Missed meal / unusual food	
Loss of appetite		Hormonal Changes	
Other:		Other:	
Other:		Other:	

Date: ______ ***Weather:*** ______

Hours Slept: ______ Insomnia? Yes ☐ No ☐

How did you feel on waking today? I felt refreshed: ☐

Slightly unrefreshed: ☐ Moderately unrefreshed: ☐ Severely unrefreshed: ☐

Did you exercise today? Yes ☐ No ☐ ______

		Morning	Afternoon	Evening
	3			
	2			
	1			
Fatigue	0			
	3			
	2			
	1			
Pain Levels	0			
	3			
	2			
	1			
Cognitive Symptoms / Brain Fog	0			

		Morning	Afternoon	Evening
	3			
	2			
	1			
Anxiety / Low Mood	0			
	3			
	2			
	1			
Activity Levels	0			
	3			
	2			
	1			
Other	0			

Symptom Score: 0 = No problem, 1 = Slight, 2 = Moderate, 3 = Severe. See p.3

Today's Notes:

Pain Location & Levels

Shade bodies, tick boxes or use pain score.

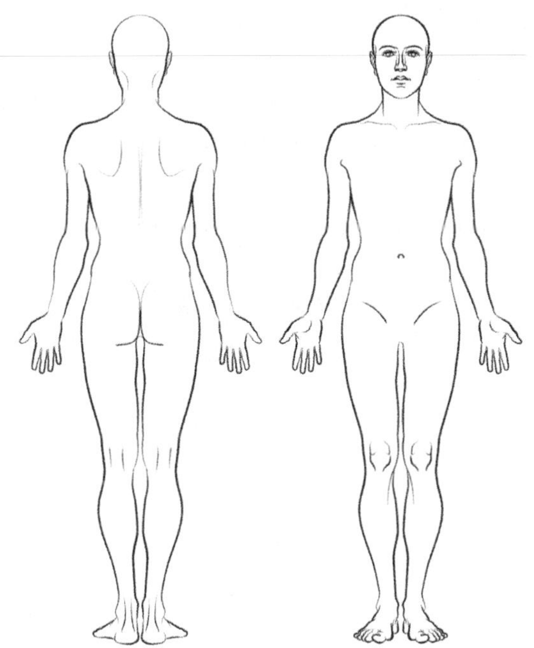

Pain Score
1 = Slight, 2 = Moderate, 3 = Severe.

	Left	Right
Jaw		
Neck		
Shoulder Girdle		
Chest		
Upper Back		
Lower Back		
Upper Arm		
Lower Arm		
Abdomen		
Hip / Buttock		
Upper Leg		
Lower Leg		

Notes

Today I Experienced			
Headache / Migraine		Diarrhoea	
Muscle Twinges / Cramps		Constipation	
Muscle Weakness		Bloating / Stomach Pain / IBS	
Skin Itching / Burning / Hives / Rash (circle all that apply)		Bladder Issues	
Bruising		Swelling	
Sweating		Stress	
Nervousness		Nausea / vomiting	
Sensitive to Sensory Stimulation (light / noise / temperature)		Numbness / Tingling (name part of body)	
Dizziness		Missed meal / unusual food	
Loss of appetite		Hormonal Changes	
Other:		Other:	
Other:		Other:	

Date: ***Weather:***

Hours Slept: Insomnia? Yes ☐ No ☐

How did you feel on waking today? I felt refreshed: ☐

Slightly unrefreshed: ☐ Moderately unrefreshed: ☐ Severely unrefreshed: ☐

Did you exercise today? Yes ☐ No ☐

		Morning	Afternoon	Evening
	3			
	2			
	1			
Fatigue	0			
	3			
	2			
	1			
Pain Levels	0			
	3			
	2			
	1			
Cognitive Symptoms / Brain Fog	0			

		Morning	Afternoon	Evening
	3			
	2			
	1			
Anxiety / Low Mood	0			
	3			
	2			
	1			
Activity Levels	0			
	3			
	2			
	1			
Other	0			

Symptom Score: 0 = No problem, 1 = Slight, 2 = Moderate, 3 = Severe. See p.3

Today's Notes:

Pain Location & Levels

Shade bodies, tick boxes or use pain score.

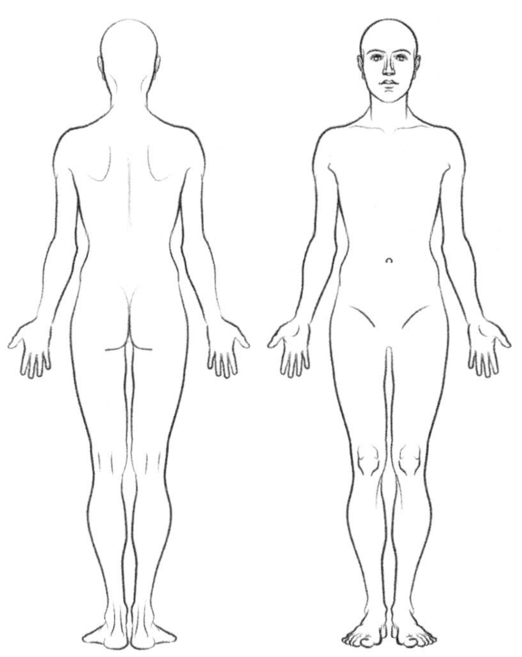

Pain Score
1 = Slight, 2 = Moderate, 3 = Severe.

	Left	Right
Jaw		
Neck		
Shoulder Girdle		
Chest		
Upper Back		
Lower Back		
Upper Arm		
Lower Arm		
Abdomen		
Hip / Buttock		
Upper Leg		
Lower Leg		

Notes

Today I Experienced			
Headache / Migraine		Diarrhoea	
Muscle Twinges / Cramps		Constipation	
Muscle Weakness		Bloating / Stomach Pain / IBS	
Skin Itching / Burning / Hives / Rash (circle all that apply)		Bladder Issues	
Bruising		Swelling	
Sweating		Stress	
Nervousness		Nausea / vomiting	
Sensitive to Sensory Stimulation (light / noise / temperature)		Numbness / Tingling (name part of body)	
Dizziness		Missed meal / unusual food	
Loss of appetite		Hormonal Changes	
Other:		Other:	
Other:		Other:	

Date: ***Weather:***

Hours Slept: Insomnia? Yes ☐ No ☐

How did you feel on waking today? I felt refreshed: ☐

Slightly unrefreshed: ☐ Moderately unrefreshed: ☐ Severely unrefreshed: ☐

Did you exercise today? Yes ☐ No ☐

		Morning	Afternoon	Evening
	3			
	2			
	1			
Fatigue	0			
	3			
	2			
	1			
Pain Levels	0			
	3			
	2			
	1			
Cognitive Symptoms / Brain Fog	0			

		Morning	Afternoon	Evening
	3			
	2			
	1			
Anxiety / Low Mood	0			
	3			
	2			
	1			
Activity Levels	0			
	3			
	2			
	1			
Other	0			

Symptom Score: 0 = No problem, 1 = Slight, 2 = Moderate, 3 = Severe. See p.3

Today's Notes:

Pain Location & Levels

Shade bodies, tick boxes or use pain score.

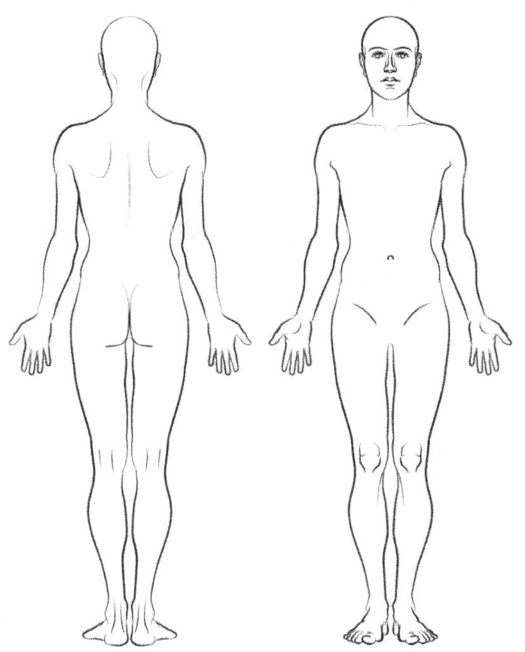

Pain Score
1 = Slight, 2 = Moderate, 3 = Severe.

	Left	Right
Jaw		
Neck		
Shoulder Girdle		
Chest		
Upper Back		
Lower Back		
Upper Arm		
Lower Arm		
Abdomen		
Hip / Buttock		
Upper Leg		
Lower Leg		

Notes

Today I Experienced			
Headache / Migraine		Diarrhoea	
Muscle Twinges / Cramps		Constipation	
Muscle Weakness		Bloating / Stomach Pain / IBS	
Skin Itching / Burning / Hives / Rash (circle all that apply)		Bladder Issues	
Bruising		Swelling	
Sweating		Stress	
Nervousness		Nausea / vomiting	
Sensitive to Sensory Stimulation (light / noise / temperature)		Numbness / Tingling (name part of body)	
Dizziness		Missed meal / unusual food	
Loss of appetite		Hormonal Changes	
Other:		Other:	
Other:		Other:	

Date: ***Weather:***

Hours Slept: Insomnia? Yes ☐ No ☐

How did you feel on waking today? I felt refreshed: ☐

Slightly unrefreshed: ☐ Moderately unrefreshed: ☐ Severely unrefreshed: ☐

Did you exercise today? Yes ☐ No ☐

		Morning	Afternoon	Evening
Fatigue	3			
	2			
	1			
	0			
Pain Levels	3			
	2			
	1			
	0			
Cognitive Symptoms / Brain Fog	3			
	2			
	1			
	0			

		Morning	Afternoon	Evening
Anxiety / Low Mood	3			
	2			
	1			
	0			
Activity Levels	3			
	2			
	1			
	0			
Other	3			
	2			
	1			
	0			

Symptom Score: 0 = No problem, 1 = Slight, 2 = Moderate, 3 = Severe. See p.3

Today's Notes:

Pain Location & Levels

Shade bodies, tick boxes or use pain score.

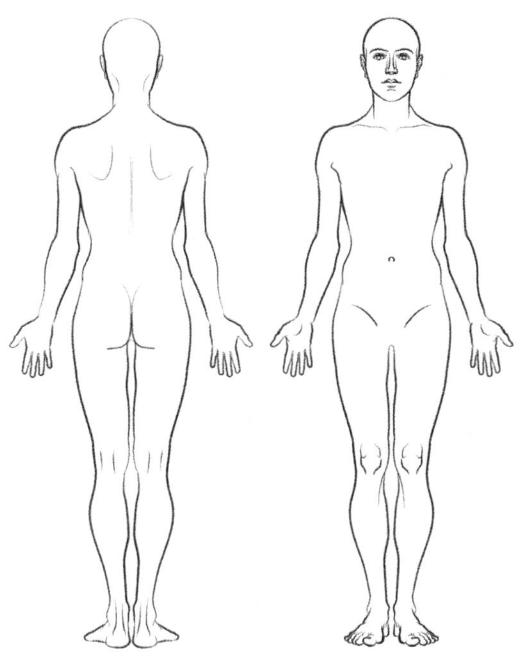

Pain Score
1 = Slight, 2 = Moderate, 3 = Severe.

	Left	Right
Jaw		
Neck		
Shoulder Girdle		
Chest		
Upper Back		
Lower Back		
Upper Arm		
Lower Arm		
Abdomen		
Hip / Buttock		
Upper Leg		
Lower Leg		

Notes

Today I Experienced			
Headache / Migraine		Diarrhoea	
Muscle Twinges / Cramps		Constipation	
Muscle Weakness		Bloating / Stomach Pain / IBS	
Skin Itching / Burning / Hives / Rash (circle all that apply)		Bladder Issues	
Bruising		Swelling	
Sweating		Stress	
Nervousness		Nausea / vomiting	
Sensitive to Sensory Stimulation (light / noise / temperature)		Numbness / Tingling (name part of body)	
Dizziness		Missed meal / unusual food	
Loss of appetite		Hormonal Changes	
Other:		Other:	
Other:		Other:	

Date: ***Weather:***

Hours Slept: Insomnia? Yes ☐ No ☐

How did you feel on waking today? I felt refreshed: ☐

Slightly unrefreshed: ☐ Moderately unrefreshed: ☐ Severely unrefreshed: ☐

Did you exercise today? Yes ☐ No ☐

		Morning	Afternoon	Evening
	3			
	2			
	1			
Fatigue	0			
	3			
	2			
	1			
Pain Levels	0			
	3			
	2			
	1			
Cognitive Symptoms / Brain Fog	0			

		Morning	Afternoon	Evening
	3			
	2			
	1			
Anxiety / Low Mood	0			
	3			
	2			
	1			
Activity Levels	0			
	3			
	2			
	1			
Other	0			

Symptom Score: 0 = No problem, 1 = Slight, 2 = Moderate, 3 = Severe. See p.3

Today's Notes:

Pain Location & Levels

Shade bodies, tick boxes or use pain score.

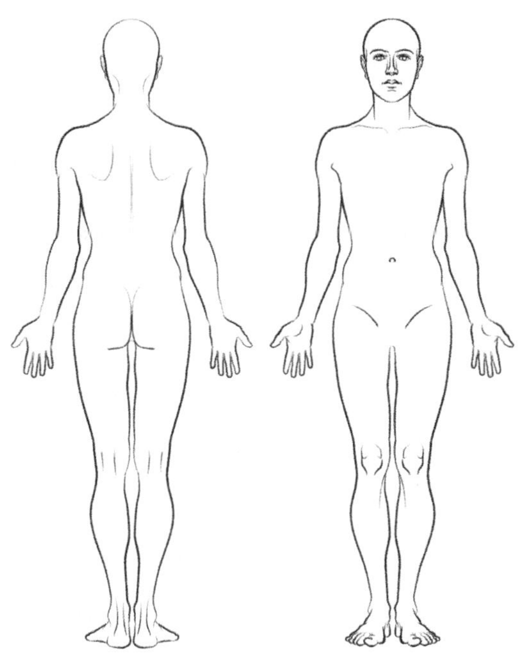

Pain Score
1 = Slight, 2 = Moderate, 3 = Severe.

	Left	Right
Jaw		
Neck		
Shoulder Girdle		
Chest		
Upper Back		
Lower Back		
Upper Arm		
Lower Arm		
Abdomen		
Hip / Buttock		
Upper Leg		
Lower Leg		

Notes

Today I Experienced			
Headache / Migraine		Diarrhoea	
Muscle Twinges / Cramps		Constipation	
Muscle Weakness		Bloating / Stomach Pain / IBS	
Skin Itching / Burning / Hives / Rash (circle all that apply)		Bladder Issues	
Bruising		Swelling	
Sweating		Stress	
Nervousness		Nausea / vomiting	
Sensitive to Sensory Stimulation (light / noise / temperature)		Numbness / Tingling (name part of body)	
Dizziness		Missed meal / unusual food	
Loss of appetite		Hormonal Changes	
Other:		Other:	
Other:		Other:	

Made in United States
North Haven, CT
27 December 2023

46675345R00122